Immigration & Assimilation

- A Hungarian Model –

Donald L Johnson

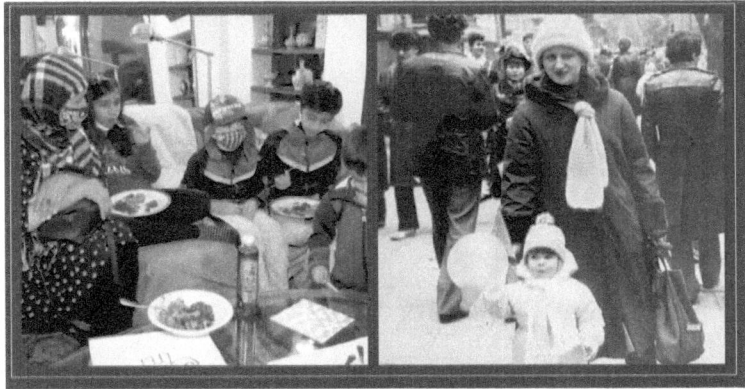

Contents

Introduction 1
The 2024 Election Through the Eyes of Patriotic Refugees 4
Applying for Citizenship in the United States 12
Some thoughts of our founding fathers 13
Some stories of immigrants from Hungary 15
    Adam von Dioszeghy 15
    Charlie Budai 17
    Gabriel Harkay 23
    Gabriel Pall 24
    Thomas Peterffy 32
    Tom Lantos: From Forced Labor to the US Congress 38
    Andrew Grove: Co-founder and CEO of Intel Corp 41
From Starvation in Ukraine to Success in Montana 47
From Liberia -- Meet the Mayor of Helena Montana 62
From Cuba (one among many) 69
Cuban family celebrates 61 years of freedom in America 72
From Communist China 80
From the Communist Chinese Cultural Revolution 82
From Congo – In Helena Montana 86
From Congo - New Haven Remembers Semi Semi-Dikoko .. 89
From Vietnam – The Lucky Few ---the Rest of the Story ... 111
Another Viet Nam Immigrant 116
From Romania 121
From Turkey 126
From North Korea 128
From Yugoslavia (where's that?) 130
Afghan doctor's family endures Taliban beatings 133
Afghanistan - again 137
From Ukraine as a child. 142
Boat People 146
Stockton farmworker turned astronaut inspires 149
Tales of my immigrant Swedish grandmother 154
Ethnic Butte Montana 170
About the author 172

Introduction

America has been called "*an exceptional nation.*" The many stories contained in this book vividly illustrate this. And in doing this book (and others) I have come to understand that the reason we are "*an exceptional nation*" is summarized by two words: Liberty & Opportunity.

Liberty spawns Opportunity.

In these stories you will see people coming from a place of little or no Liberty, thus little or no Opportunity. Then when they arrive on the shores of America where there is much Liberty, they are offered much Opportunity, and thus success and contributions in many ways.

Immigration is much in the news these days, both here in the U.S. and in Europe, and a huge political football in both places with many violent crimes and sexual assaults being committed in countries such as Sweden and Germany.

The United States from its inception is an immigrant nation, and as many of us can attest, our roots are in the forefathers who immigrated here whether in the present or in the distant past. For example, in my own hometown of Butte Montana, a mining town that attracted people from all over the world, NO SMOKING signs in the mines were posted in 14 different languages.

The success or failure of a society such as ours tracks closely to the assimilation of those disparate immigrant people into the culture of the nation, and for the most part, this assimilation has been quite successful – often after much struggle as in the case of the Irish and the Italians. But through assimilation, each new immigrant population has entered into the fabric of America, and often with significant contributions.

The stories of refugees from the 1956 Hungarian Revolution and elsewhere around the world provide inspiring stories of struggle, survival, perseverance and success. Some I have knowledge of provide a model of what immigration and assimilation should be.

The short lived and tragic Hungarian Revolution was the first rip in the Iron Curtain. Virtually all segments of Hungarian culture rebelled against the communist government and their Soviet masters; students, factory workers, farmers, police, military and even some of the top Hungarian leaders.

Many 10s of thousands fled to the West. Many of these were the best Hungary had, and as they assimilated into the West, in particular into the United States, many made significant contributions to the culture of their new nation. I have known some of these.

But Hungary is only one of the many nations from which immigrants have come to the United States, many of them refugees from tyrannical nations and from war torn nations. I have included here a few such stories of such naturalized American citizens. They come from communist China, communist Cuba, and a refugee from war torn Libera who is currently the Mayor of Helena Montana. How is that possible given that the black population in Montana and in Helena Montana is less than 1%.

This book is one of several I have authored centering on refugee immigrants and their impact on American life:

- Yearning for Liberty, A look at the cost and value of liberty.
- The Life and Times of Adam von Dioszeghy – Hungarian Freedom Fighter A veteran of WW-II, the Hungarian revolution of 1956, and Vietnam – and a friend.
- *The Freymans: An Intimate Look Into an Extraordinary 20th Century Family* The story of a family member whose family escaped from Latvia during World War II.

The 2024 Election Through the Eyes of Patriotic Refugees

Ref: The 2024 Election Through the Eyes of Patriotic Refugees - The Stream

I include this article because of importance of proper immigration in this election, and what illegal immigration is doing to this nation which has historically extended a welcoming hand to legal immigrants.

The glaring and destructive hypocrisy of Joe Biden is seen here as written here by the daughter of Vietnamese parents who escaped from the North Vietnam onslaught in April 1975. Biden at the time was willing to cast tens of thousands of desperate South Vietnamese allies to the slaughter and slavery of the communist North Vietnamese, much the same as he did later with Afghanistan allies in the disastrous evacuation of Afghanistan in 2021.

Later, this same man, then a US Senator, now a US President opened the US borders allowing millions of unvetted individuals into the US homeland with no regard as to who they are and what they agenda they may have. No doubt some may may contribute much to American society and culture in coming years, but there are those who even now are demonstrating criminal and destructive activity.

President Biden's open border immigration policies earn him much shame and are an affront to the many people highlighted in the pages to follow.

Flickr/USMC Archives

> *Michele Le is a litigator who advocates for the strengthening of the Western Church. You can read her reflections on current political and social issues on the Substack: Of Serpents + Doves*

Politics were not discussed in the house where I grew up.

I used to think it was strange that my parents didn't talk about their escape from war-torn South Vietnam. Instead, they focused on making sure that my brothers and I worked hard in school so we could maximize the blessings of living in this country.

So I was surprised when my mother, who was in her sixties, first told me about her experience with communism in Vietnam. I sat at my parents' kitchen table, agape as she described the day the Viet Cong invaded her neighborhood. She watched her father frantically load her young siblings into his South Vietnamese government Jeep while under fire by bloodthirsty communists. He was forced by the barrage of bullets to leave her, 15 years old at the time, and her mother behind. They were forced to flee on foot, dodging bullets from the Communists' rifles.

My mother and grandmother survived this event, but the communists would strike many more times against their family in the coming years.

My parents' harrowing escape from Vietnam in April 1975 is etched into their psyches. Their suffering was not merely because of the dangers of floating out on a rickety boat into the dark South China Sea teeming with pirates hellbent on robbing, raping, and killing refugees. It was the guilt and fear of never again laying eyes on the loved ones left behind. It was also the knowledge that their ancestral homeland was lost forever.

But my parents are among the lucky ones who were rescued by the U.S. Navy's Seventh Fleet. They were fished out of the sea and eventually given refuge in America due to the concerted efforts of President Gerald Ford and evangelist Billy Graham. Though there had been a bipartisan effort to pass legislation that would allow and fund the evacuation and resettlement of the South Vietnamese refugees in America, noteworthy opponents in the Senate Foreign Relations Committee made public statements like, **"We owe no obligation, moral or otherwise, to evacuate foreign nationals."**

It did not matter to then-Senator Joe Biden that more than 170,000 South Vietnamese people who had worked hand-in-hand with the U.S. military were in danger of losing their lives if they were not evacuated. Biden ignored this reality and went on to emphasize that "the United States has no obligation to evacuate one – or 100,001 – South Vietnamese."

Communist America

Those heartless sentiments will never be forgotten by the South Vietnamese who managed to survive the Vietnam War. But they serve as potent motivation for these legal migrants to assimilate into the American culture, gain citizenship, and prove their worth to those who fought for their safe passage and settlement in this great nation.

My parents' gratitude and loyalty to America compels them now to speak of the dangers they see threatening this constitutional republic. Every day they see the rise of communism in their adopted homeland. When my parents came to this country, they knew they had been given a blessing by Almighty God. No other country holds the promise of human flourishing so reliably as the United States of America. There would be no need to worry about the government taking citizens to jail in the dead of night for political dissent. There would be no need to worry that private property would be unilaterally taken without compensation, as was common in North Vietnam and post-war communist South Vietnam. There would be no need to hide their religious convictions in this pluralistic American society.

But their eyes and ears do not lie. Communism has crept into America like a wolf in sheep's clothing. Democracy is no longer about "government of the people, by the people, for the people." The word "democracy" has now been misappropriated by powerful elites ensconced in American colleges, multinational corporations, the legacy media, the entertainment industry, and our own government to mask their strategies to maintain power indefinitely. Why else do those in power seek to jail their political opponents for questionable "crimes," censor free speech, curtail the right to bear arms, "pack" the

Supreme Court, "pack" the Senate, circumvent a primary process intended to allow the people to choose their presidential candidates, abolish the Electoral College, abolish the congressional filibuster, disallow voter ID, import millions of illegal aliens and encourage them to vote?

These are the means of maintaining the power of the communist vanguard party, not how democracy is preserved. But these elites are not after a classless society à la communism. No. They have learned the lessons of history. They know that people can be fraudulently led to believe that a whole community can "own" all the means of production and that private property can be equitably distributed to the people.

The reality of communism is that private property is stolen from the masses and kept by the elite few. Crumbs are handed out to the fools who fall for the mask of equity. Among the losers in this battle are those who remain silent as the evil elite rise to power.

The Only Way to Win

What now? What can be done? Today, the only solution is for Christians to pray up, stand up, speak up, and be heard. It begins with each of us daring to ask God how we can shine His light into the darkness permeating our culture and government. Scripture tells us that the "days are evil," that we are being "sent out as sheep in the midst of wolves," and that we will need to be "clever as serpents and pure as doves." We are not to be "conformed to this evil world" but rather that we are to fight "against the rulers, against the authorities, against the powers of this dark world."

At a minimum, this Christian duty to fight evil requires that we exercise our right to vote. This means that we vote even when our choices are between two sinful candidates, because there will never be a sinless politician. Moses was a murderer before he was tasked by God to lead the Israelites out of slavery. The Apostle Paul persecuted Christians before he met Jesus on the road to Damascus. Demonstrably, our Lord repeatedly uses imperfect people to execute His will. So our vote must be based on our obedience to the Word of God; we must carefully consider and compare the policies and platforms of the candidates and parties to discern which most closely align with God's will and His righteous laws as expressed in the Bible. In this way, we can ensure that the values most closely aligned with God's values will be enshrined in the law of the land.

Please Support *The Stream*: Equipping Christians to Think Clearly About the Political, Economic, and Moral Issues of Our Day.

Our political involvement is one of the most effective ways that we can ensure the welfare of those Jesus Christ described as "the least of these" – the poor, the vulnerable, the stranger, the naked, the sick, and the imprisoned. My refugee parents were among the least of these. But for the righteous morals of the politicians in office in 1975, pressing forward despite heavy opposition, my parents and hundreds of thousands of other refugees would have languished in communist concentration camps or perished at sea.

But there are yet more of "the least of these" that need our political action: the unborn – knit together in their mothers' wombs by God, yet torn asunder by man; children led into sexual immorality with pornography in public schools; children encouraged to permanently sterilize and mutilate their bodies in defiance of God's ordination of the binary sexes; parents of these exploited children who've been stripped of their legal authority to save them; women and children trafficked by deviants allowed into our country through a porous national border; traumatized and injured veterans left on the streets; the abandoned citizens of North Carolina who have lost everything in Hurricane Helene; and the millions of hard-working Americans who can't make ends meet because of the games politicians have played with our currency.

And let us not forget that God's people have also been among the persecuted in this country. Since 1954, the Johnson Amendment of the federal tax code has been used to muzzle religious leaders from speaking on political issues for fear of losing their churches' tax exemptions. The blatant discrimination was further demonstrated during the COVID pandemic when churches and synagogues were forbidden from opening their doors while liquor stores and strip clubs were considered "essential businesses."

How We Got Here

How have these things all happened in America, you may wonder? I cannot offer a complete explanation, but one thing is clear: The Church as a whole has largely looked on passively as Adam did while Eve spoke with the serpent in Genesis. Scripture and the wise words of G.K. Chesterton make clear what befalls a man who is silent in the face of evil: "Unless a man becomes the enemy of an evil, he will not even become its slave but rather its champion."

Perhaps the Johnson Amendment is what understandably makes pastors leery of preaching about political matters. But I submit to you that all matters of morality are also political. Politics and morality are necessarily intertwined, as each is useless without the other. This is evident from God's declarations of laws and establishment and destruction of rulers and nations.

If pastors are confused or leery, we should encourage and pray for them so they acquire the clarity and courage of the apostles as they set out across the ancient world. In the meantime, we, the Body of Christ, should not be timid, but lovingly speak the truth, vote, and fear not the judgment of men. Rather we should fear God's judgment.

A unified Christian vote can deal a mighty blow against the evil holding sway in the world. But a divided Church – one that fails to "seek first His kingdom and His righteousness" – allows evil to spread and grasp more power.

This is what happened to Adam in the Garden of Eden. His first sin was not eating the forbidden fruit; it was failing to focus on God's will as he silently watched Eve be tempted by the enemy and then fooled into sinful action.

As we cast our ballots in the 2024 election, let us set our eyes on God's righteousness, and thereby prove that we have learned from Adam's devastating mistake.

Applying for Citizenship in the United States

A search for what is involved in seeking "legal" immigration into the United States of America yields:

- You already have a green card.
- You are at least 18 years old.
- You have lived in the U.S. lawfully as a permanent resident for at least five years <u>unless</u> you are a spouse of a U.S. citizen, refugee, or received your green card through political asylum.
- During those five years, you have been physically present in the U.S. for at least half of the time.
- You have not spent more than one year at a time outside the U.S.
- You have not established a primary home in another country.
- You have lived in the state or district where you are filing your application for at least three months.
- You have "good moral character."
- You can read, write and speak English.
- You can pass a test about U.S. history and government.
- You will swear that you believe in the principles of the U.S. Constitution and will be loyal to the U.S.

The intent of this sometimes long and difficult naturalization process is to gain some measure of assurance, for both the applicant and the nation, that the applicant will assimilate successfully as a US citizen. Such assurance most likely will be severely lacking for those entering the nation illegally.

Some thoughts of our founding fathers

When we are considering the advantages that may result from an easy mode of naturalization, we ought also to consider the cautions necessary to guard against abuses. It is no doubt very desirable that we should hold out as many inducements as possible for the worthy part of mankind to come and settle amongst us, and throw their fortunes into a common lot with ours. But why is this desirable? Not merely to swell the catalogue of people. No, sir, it is to increase the wealth and strength of the community; and those who acquire the rights of citizenship without adding to the strength or wealth of the community are not the people we are in want of ... I should be exceedingly sorry, sir, that our rule of naturalization excluded a single person of good fame that really meant to incorporate himself into our society; on the other hand, I do not wish that any man should acquire the privilege, but such as would be a real addition to the wealth or strength of the United States.

James Madison - 1790

The safety of a republic depends essentially on the energy of a common National sentiment; on a uniformity of principles and habits; on the exemption of the citizens from foreign bias, and prejudice; and on that love of country which will almost invariably be found to be closely connected with birth, education and family.

Alexander Hamilton - 1802

Against the insidious wiles of foreign influence, I conjure you to believe me, fellow-citizens, the jealousy of a free people ought to be constantly awake, since history and experience prove that foreign influence is one of the most baneful foes of republican Government.

George Washington - 1796

Everywhere immigrants have enriched and strengthened the fabric of American life.

John F. Kennedy

Some stories of immigrants from Hungary

Adam von Dioszeghy

(**Mr. von D** – as he was known by his US Navy shipmates) is a survivor of the World War II battle of Budapest – a battle pitting the air forces of Great Britain and the United States, the German occupying army and the Soviet Red Army – all converging around the basement bomb shelter where seven year old Adam and his mother survive against this harrowing onslaught.

Surviving the war, they suffered in the following years under the brutal oppression of Communist rule.

In 1956 young Adam became involved in the revolution and was twice wounded. The revolution was brutally squashed by the Red Army and Adam and his mother were marked for death and escaped in the dead of night to Austria with nothing but the clothes they were wearing and little usable cash.

Adam and his mother eventually made their way to Menlo Park California where Adam earned a degree from Stanford University. Mind you, that when the two of them first arrived in America they spoke no English.

Adam was then called up in the draft in the early years of the Vietnam War and joined the Navy and was commissioned an officer in the US Navy and assigned to the World War II Fletcher Class destroyer USS Porterfield where we served side by side at General Quarters and on the bridge during normal underway operations.

Following Navy service with three tours to Vietnam, Adam returned to Stanford where he earned a law degree and practiced as a trial lawyer for many years in Northern California.

I hooked up with Mr. von D again in recent months (Spring 2016) when I discovered him via the internet. Adam and his wife retired a few years back, and at his wife's suggestion, have returned to live in and around Budapest once more – his wife was born and raised in Northern California.

In May 2017 my wife and I traveled to Hungary where, after 50+ years, Adam and I, along with our wives, had a reunion of two old Navy shipmates. During this week Adam shared much of his early years, including a walking tour of the Budapest of his youth. This tour took us to his Budapest apartment and his neighborhood of World War II where we peeked into his basement bomb shelter. The tour then took us to the places of the 1956 revolution. During this tour I listened carefully and took many pictures. I then composed a book for Adam – Budapest at War - which is available at my on-line book store.

Adam and his wife Aliz have now written and published three books. Search in Amazon for "von Dioszeghy" and find these fascinating books.

Charlie Budai

Like Mr. von D — Charlie was a Hungarian refugee and experienced many of the same things in surviving WW-II as a young child ... living under a brutal Communist regime ... escaping a crushed revolution ... and finally resettling and assimilating into the American culture. We met Joan, the widow of Charlie, a few years ago, but never knew Charlie. She told a spell binding story of how she and her husband met and married. I later asked if any of this had been written down. She responded by sending unpublished stories of their life together, including an extensive account of Charlie's life growing up in Hungary through WW-II, the oppression of the Communist years and his involvement in the revolution and subsequent escape to the West and the US.

Several episodes highlight the heritage of Charlie and the type of man that came to America in 1956:

First are his descriptions of his mother hiding Polish Jews from the Germans who were bent on the extermination of all Jews. His mother did this at the risk of her own life as well as the lives of her family.

Second is Charlie learning English in America by spending many hours in movie theaters, often watching the same movies over and over and with a dictionary and a pad and pencil at hand.

Another came about somewhat casually as we were visiting Charlie's wife at her home. I commented on the flag flying at the property entrance and visible from the front window. Yes, she said, Charlie always liked to have the American flag flying where he could see it. This to me was a great testimony of how this refugee from war and tyranny viewed his new home country.

I've read Charlie's story and have published it in book form for Joan and her family and friends. It is indeed captivating and inspiring. The story is very well written – and from one who knew no English when he entered the US as a refugee — rest assured that Charlie assimilated into the American culture and became a productive citizen in his new country. It is an inspiring story of overcoming war, an oppressive government, revolution and crafting a new and successful life in a free society.

Charlie's story

Diana and I visited Joan in the fall of 2025, and she invited us to an annual Hungarian potluck. It was there that we solidified our affinity for the Hungarian freedom fighters and their stories. There were 28 of us Hungarians, and it was a joy to mingle and get to know some of them. Two were of the first generation of those freedom fighters, and others were second generation, including Charlie's and Joan's son and daughter.

I listened in on a conversation between two of the second-generation men. They were lamenting the deterioration of the work ethic among younger generation Americans. What I took from this interchange was that these men learned from their fathers (Freedom Fighters) the value that American liberty offered to all that would partake of that liberty, and the responsibility that goes along with those opportunities.

It was at this gathering that Joan introduced her and Charlie's book. Joan has also written the story of her and Charlie's life together and asked that I make this into a book for her, so this will be a winter project for me.

Gabriel Harkay

I knew **_Gabriel Harkay_** and worked with him at Cubic Corp back in the 1980s. He was quite a good civil engineer and worked many projects around the world building communications towers and facilities for our Tactical Aircrew Training System . I wish I had paid more attention to Gabe back then, but I do know that he was a refugee from the 1956 Hungarian revolution, and likely had experiences similar to others I have written about.

One project we worked together was a system for the Iranian Air Force in the late 1970s. We were scheduled to deploy to Iran to install the system in early 1980, and Gabe was in Tehran doing some preparatory work. The revolutionaries stormed the hotel where Gabe was staying, broke all of the liquor bottles in the first-floor bar and set it all on fire, cutting off escape of guests in the rooms above. Fortunately, there was a construction tower adjacent to the hotel and guests were lifted from the roof of the burning hotel to the tower and to safety. So inadvertently Gabe Harkay was involved in his second revolution and survived both. Needless to say, we did not deploy the system to Iran.

I regret not having details of my friend Gabe's life, and I've since found that Gabe has passed.

Gabriel Pall is another fascinating story I stumbled on:

Chance encounter in war-torn Hungary renewed 64 years later

Yet another interesting and inspiring refugee from Hungary. An American B-24 bomber was forced to crash land in Hungary after a bombing mission. Bob Holcomb was the bombardier on that mission, and after the unplanned landing a group of young and curious Hungarian boys gathered around the aircraft and its crew. Among the boys was Gabriel Pall who spoke a little English, and the two struck up a very brief friendship.

Like other local children, young Gabriel was drawn to the U.S. airmen like a magnet.

Holcomb had some candy in his pockets and gave some to the young boy, told him his name and said '*If you ever get to America ... look me up*'

Mr. Pall did come to the States — in 1957 following the 1956 revolution, and like the others I've found, assimilated into the American culture and led a productive and quite remarkable professional life.

And Mr. Pall was tenacious in finding his American of years past and he and Mr. Holcomb met again after a long 64 years. For Pall, their meeting left a lasting impression as evidenced by the tenacity in which he searched those many decades for his American flyboy friend.

"I remember two things," Pall said. "One, he gave me Wrigley's chewing gum. And two, he said, '*Hey, kid – if you ever get to America, look me up.*'"

Holcomb and the rest of his bomber crew made their way to Budapest and then back to Italy ... and finally back home to America.

Pall escaped from Soviet-dominated Hungary in 1956 to start a new life in America.

Gabriel Pall with his wife, Christine Rose, left, and their daughter, Laura Rose, at Laura's graduation from the University of Virginia.

Pall grew up under the Soviet-backed communist regime in Hungary. His family moved to Budapest, where he attended high school and enrolled in college to study civil engineering. In 1956, he graduated from the Technical University of Budapest. He went to work for the government, designing state rail and highway projects, and began training as a reserve officer with the Hungarian army corps of engineers.

Then came Oct. 23 that year, and the Hungarian Revolution. After a brief, heady taste of independence, the Soviet armored divisions rolled across the border and crushed the rebellion.

Hungary's Stalinist government had been repressive before the uprising, Pall said, but now, he knew, it would be even worse. He and his fiancée, Agnes Szabo, decided they would try to get out.

On Nov. 23, the couple left Budapest by train for Szombathely, only 20 miles from Austria and freedom. But the railroad station was surrounded by Soviet troops and local militias, checking identity papers and arresting anyone without a residency permit.

They were trapped.

A local resident warned them of armed Soviet patrols and showed them where to hide, promising to send a guide after nightfall. The man showed up as promised and took them to a house at the edge of town, where a small group of refugees was waiting to cross into Austria.

They walked several miles across open fields, not speaking, wrapped in bed sheets to blend into the snow-covered countryside. When they arrived at the frontier, they found it guarded by barbed wire and landmines.

Using knitting needles to probe the ground, Pall and the guide painstakingly marked a safe path through the minefield. As the group began to cross, flares lit up the night and machinegun fire shredded the silence. The guide ordered everyone to drop to the ground.

They were lucky. The border guards hadn't seen them — they were shooting at someone else. After the gunfire stopped, they completed their journey into Austria, where they found safe haven at a place called Lutzmannsburg.

Later, they learned that another group of refugees had been gunned down by a patrol a mile or two from their crossing point.

'If you ever get to America ...'

Gabriel Pall and Agnes Szabo found a warm welcome in Austria, and the couple got married in Vienna on Dec. 27, 1956. But Pall never intended to stay there forever.

"I had this destination, which was to come to America," he said.

He had an uncle in the States and, he thought, a friend in Oregon – that dashing young flyboy he had met during the war.

The next year, under an Eisenhower-era program designed to recruit engineering talent fleeing Soviet-bloc countries, the couple secured a visa and crossed the pond.

They settled in Philadelphia, where Pall began a long and successful career with IBM. He rose through the corporate ranks, taking ever more challenging assignments with the company. In 1983, Agnes died of cancer. Pall remarried, and his new wife gave birth to a daughter. He retired from IBM, did some consulting, then accepted a faculty position at the College of William & Mary.

Gabriel Pall: Some Background Information

- Member American Society of Civil Engineers
- Member Association for Computing Machinery.
- Member American Society for Quality
- Member American Society for Training and Development

Education

- BS degree
  Structural Engineering
  Technical University of Budapest
- MS degree
  Engineering Mechanics
  University of Pennsylvania

A fitting conclusion to this story of Gabriel Pall is the following news article:

WILLIAMSBURG, Va., March 11, 2014 – A Citizenship Ceremony for children of recently naturalized United States citizens will be held on Saturday, March 22, at Jamestown Settlement, a museum of 17th-century Virginia. The event is hosted by the Williamsburg Chapter National Society Daughters of the American Revolution (NSDAR) and the Jamestown-Yorktown Foundation in partnership with U.S. Citizenship and Immigration Services (USCIS) of the Department of Homeland Security.

Fifty young people ages 11 to 25 from 26 countries – Belarus, Benin, Canada, China, Cuba, Dominican Republic, Egypt, Ethiopia, Germany, Ghana, Greece, India, Republic of Kazakhstan, Kenya, Kosovo, Lithuania, Mauritius, Mexico, Panama, Philippines, Romania, Russia, Sudan, United Kingdom, Ukraine and

Vietnam – will take the Oath of Allegiance to the United States and receive formal acknowledgement of their citizenship. The ceremony begins at 2 p.m. and is open to the public on a space-available basis.

"We are proud to join with the Jamestown-Yorktown Foundation and USCIS to sponsor this truly special ceremony for a third year," said Jane M. Stewart, regent for the Williamsburg Chapter NSDAR, which co-sponsors two adult naturalization ceremonies annually in June and December with the Colonial Williamsburg Foundation. "It's appropriate to hold it at Jamestown Settlement, near where some of the very first immigrants to our country came ashore."

Featured speaker for the event is Williamsburg resident Gabriel A. Pall, an internationally recognized author and management consultant. A native of Hungary, he escaped to Austria during the Hungarian Revolution in 1956, immigrated to the United States the following year and became a naturalized citizen in 1962. After a 30-year career with IBM, he retired as an executive and later became president of Juran International Inc., a global consulting firm specializing in quality management. More recently, Mr. Pall has consulted on project and process management with the College of William and Mary.

Finally, read this snippet from an article from a Hungarian organization in Cleveland where many of the refugees, including Charlie, lived for a time before moving on.

"These refugees were markedly different from any previous wave of Hungarian immigrants. First of all, they were the youngest group; many were single. The majority had some kind of technical training and their skills were readily employed by American industry. Psychologically, immigration made lasting impressions on these refugees. For eleven years they experienced life under economic depravity and political terror. As a direct consequence, their interests in America were more materialistic and self-centered; cultural or group attachments were much weaker when compared to those of previous waves of immigrants. **They adjusted with greater ease, learned English in a short while, with many of them marrying English-speaking mates. Their contributions to their adopted homeland were numerous."**

I am inspired by these stories, and hope you are as well. I also hope you will agree that these Hungarians represent the best possible model of immigration and assimilation.

And note that these Hungarian refugees were gathered together at an Army base in New Jersey and vetted prior to release into the general American populace – for several reasons:

Among the refugees were plants from the Soviet Union, plants whose missions included espionage against the United States, and assassinations against fellow refugees. Charlie, in his memoir, tells of the many years he spent in looking over his shoulder for that would be assassin.

1956 being at the height of the Cold War, the US was interested in conditions behind the Iron Curtain. These Hungarian refugees were interrogated in order to extract as much useful information as possible. Some such as Andrew Grove were educated in the sciences and engineering and could provide insight into the scientific and engineering maturity and capabilities of the Soviet Union. The average age of refugees was 23, including many children, well educated (from one university 500 students, 32 professors, and their families fled), and talented (including musicians, athletes, writers, engineers and other professionals) people come through swamps and guards to reach non-communist Austria. The Austrian people were exemplary in their welcome of the Hungarian refugees.

But let's not leave this story just yet – there's more:

The nation that welcomed these refugees is a big part of the story. A story that begins with the words from our Declaration of Independence

"We hold these truths to be self-evident, that all men are created equal, that they are endowed by their Creator with certain unalienable Rights, that among these are Life, Liberty and the pursuit of Happiness." and from our Constitution beginning with the words "We the People…"

It is these ideals enshrined from the very beginning in the very fabric of America that afforded these refugees the liberty and opportunity to begin new lives – lives to be lived not under the yoke of kings, queens, emperors, dictators, bishops, czars, slave holders or other autocrats. No, these new American citizens would rise or fall primarily on their own merits … and also with the benevolent help of other free citizens and the governments freely elected by free men and women. Was it easy? No. But there were no machineguns, tanks or minefields set up to dictate their every thought or movement.

These 35,000 or more freedom seeking Hungarians sought out and made new lives in that *Exceptional Nation* the United States of America.

Thomas Peterffy

And here is yet another ...

Note that **Thomas Peterffy** came out of Hungary much later than the others I've highlighted. However, he did live under the oppression of Communism in Hungary and escaped from it.

Thomas Peterffy was born in Budapest, Hungary in 1944, in a hospital basement during a Russian air raid. He left his engineering studies and emigrated to the United States as a refugee in 1965. When he moved to New York City, he did not speak English. He eventually earned a bachelor's degree from Clark University.

Peterffy began his career in the US as an architectural draftsman working on highway projects for an engineering firm. It was at this firm that he volunteered to program a newly-purchased computer, ultimately shaping the course of his future. Of his background in programming Peterffy said, "I think the way a CEO runs his company is a reflection of his background. Business is a collection of processes, and my job is to automate those processes so that they can be done with the greatest amount of efficiency."

Peterffy left his career designing financial modelling software and bought a seat on the American Stock Exchange to trade equity options. During his career in finance, he has consistently pushed to replace manual processes with more efficient automated ones. He would write code in his head during the trading day and then apply his ideas to computerized trading models after hours. Peterffy created a major stir among traders by introducing handheld computers onto the trading floor in the early 1980s. His business related to his AMEX seat eventually developed into Interactive Brokers.

Regulatory influence and political views

In 1999, Peterffy was influential in persuading the Securities and Exchange Commission (SEC) that US options markets could be linked electronically, which would ensure that investors receive the best possible options prices. He has also testified before the United States Senate Banking Subcommittee on Securities, Insurance, and Investment about adding banking regulations.

During the 2012 United States presidential campaign, Peterffy created political ads in support of the Republican Party. Peterffy bought millions of dollars of air time on networks such as CNN, CNBC, and Bloomberg. The ads consisted of a minute-long spot narrated by Peterffy that warned against creeping socialism in the United States. The ads were considered remarkable in part because Peterffy is not a candidate and did not buy the ads through a "527 group" but instead paid for them directly.

In the spot Peterffy said, "America's wealth comes from the efforts of people striving for success. Take away their incentive with badmouthing success and you take away the wealth that helps us take care of the needy. Yes, in socialism the rich will be poorer — but the poor will also be poorer. People will lose interest in really working hard and creating jobs." Peterffy did not directly mention Mitt Romney or Barack Obama, but clearly favored the former.

Peterffy's ad received mixed responses. Joshua Green, writing for *Bloomberg Businessweek*, said "The ad, while slightly ridiculous, is deeply sincere and also quite affecting". Green also asked Peterffy whether the comparison between the United States and Hungary made in the ad was a fair one: "[Peterffy] couldn't really think that the U.S. was turning into socialist Hungary, could he? The government isn't suppressing speech and throwing political opponents in jail. No, he conceded, it wasn't. But it sure feels like that's the path we're on."

https://en.wikipedia.org/wiki/Thomas_Peterffy - cite_note-Bloomberg-12

Politico reported that the ad was "being hailed as one of the best spots this election cycle", and said that it could have been influential in Ohio due to its large Hungarian population.

Voter registration records in Connecticut show that Peterffy is registered as an independent voter. Campaign contribution records show that he donated at least $60,000 to the Republican National Committee in 2011 and that over the past few years has mostly donated to Republican candidates.

During the 2016 presidential election, Peterffy donated $100,000 to the campaign of Republican nominee Donald Trump. https://en.wikipedia.org/wiki/Thomas_Peterffy - cite_note-bcoffey1-14

Hungarians know things that others in the West have only read about. They know oppression and tyranny.

Many, though certainly not all, within today's new refugees from the Middle East are merely transplanting their tyranny to new locations. But it doesn't take many to wreak havoc as seen recently in many European nations and in the United States as well.

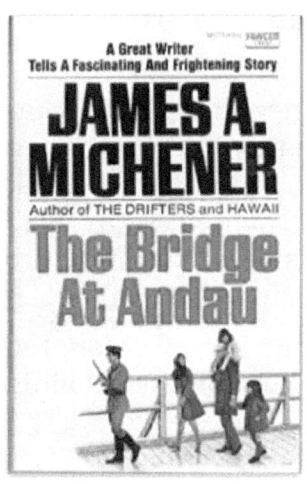

Read "The Bridge at Andau" by *James Michener*, a work of non-fiction. Yes, the Hungarians were refugees themselves and others in Europe welcomed them and many came to America. The Hungarians did not bring with them a murderous attitude to all who were not Hungarians. They did not bring with them a hatred of those who gave them shelter. They did not attack women, priests, nightclubs or newspapers. They did not fly large airplanes into large buildings nor drive trucks down the streets mowing people down. They did not behead others in the land that gave them sanctuary. They did not set off bombs at large sporting events or in shopping malls.

The Hungarian refugees of 1956-57 sought to escape oppression and avail themselves of the opportunities offered by free societies. And many have contributed in positive ways as shown by the handful I have highlighted above.

Many of the un-vetted new refugees in Europe and the US want to spread oppression and destabilize rather than contribute to their host nations in positive ways.

If we are to remain a culture valuing liberty and opportunity, and a culture gleaning the best that foreign immigrants have to offer, while providing sanctuary to those fleeing oppression, let us return to the Hungarian model. The high bar set by the Hungarians in the mid-1950s has been dramatically and deliberately lowered in recent years in the name of political expediency. We lower the bar at our own peril and risk a fundamental transformation of our nation.

And let us ponder the words of our founding fathers and their vision of what their new nation would become.

Tom Lantos: From Forced Labor to the US Congress

Member of the U.S. House of Representatives from California

Tom Lantos will be long remembered for his profound moral convictions and his deep commitment to human rights. During his life he helped and inspired numerous individuals around the world. Many more will feel the rewards of his work for years to come.

Tom was born in Budapest, Hungary, where as a teenager he was sent to a forced labor camp by the German Nazi occupant military. After escaping the labor camp, he sought refuge with an aunt who lived in a safe house operated by Raoul Wallenberg, the Swedish diplomat who used his official status and visa-issuing powers to save thousands of Hungarian Jews. Tom quickly joined the anti-Nazi resistance. After the Russians liberated Budapest in 1945, Tom tried to locate his mother and family members but came to realize that they had all perished in the Holocaust.

In 1947, Tom came to the United States to study on a Hillel Foundation Scholarship. He earned his B.A. in 1949 and M.A. in economics in 1950 both from the University of Washington in Seattle. Three years later he received a Ph.D. in economics from the University of California, Berkeley. He subsequently served as a foreign policy commentator on television and as a senior advisor to several U.S. Senators.

Elected to office in 1980, Tom rose to become Chairman of the House Committee on Foreign Affairs and one of the country's leading champions of human rights. His commitment to this issue was forged from the loss of his family during the Holocaust.

After being diagnosed with esophageal cancer in late December 2007, Congressman Lantos announced that he would not seek reelection. He said at the time,

"It is only in the United States that a penniless survivor of the Holocaust and a fighter in the anti-Nazi underground could have received an education, raised a family, and had the privilege of serving the last three decades of his life as a Member of Congress. I will never be able to express fully my profoundly felt gratitude to this great country."

LANTOS FOUNDATION, 6 DIXON AVE, SUITE 100, CONCORD, NH 03301 (603) 226-3636 INFO@LANTOSFOUNDATION.ORG

I learned of Congressman Tom Lantos from the 1999 documentary The Last Days 1. Lantos along with five Jewish Hungarians, now U.S. citizens, tell their stories: before March 1944, when Nazis began to exterminate Hungarian Jews, months in concentration camps, and visiting childhood homes more than 50 years later. An historian, a Sonderkommando, a doctor who experimented on Auschwitz prisoners, and US soldiers who were part of the liberation in April 1945, also comment. Most telling are details: Renée packing her bathing suit, Irene swallowing the diamonds her mother gave her to buy bread, Alice's memorial for her sister Klara, Bill escaping police by jumping into a line of Jews going to Buchenwald, and Tom told by a US soldier to have *"all the damn bananas and oranges you can eat."*

See the trailer of the film at: https://youtu.be/TTc-f5RxVPc

This is a hard film to watch, but these lives and the stories they tell must never be forgotten.

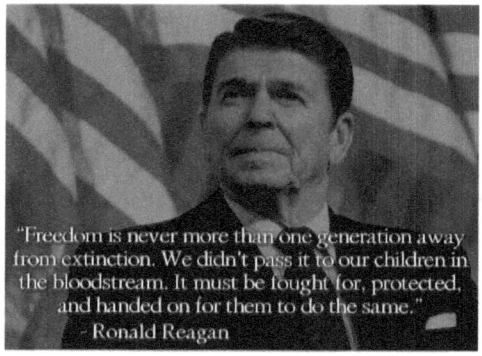

---

[1] The Last Days (1998) - Plot Summary
https://www.imdb.com/title/tt0174852/plotsummary

Andrew Grove: Co-founder and CEO of Intel Corp

Though I did not know Andy Grove personally, like many 10s of thousands I have greatly benefited from him and appreciate greatly that he escaped from Hungary in 1956. You see, Mr. Grove co-founded and was long-term CEO of Intel Corporation. I have been using his products for a number of years, including right now as I am researching, composing and publishing this book using an Intel computer chip – all while listening to music, catching up on the events of the day and looking for that next great soup recipe. .

Andrew Grove was one of many who escaped from that revolution. Many such as Grove were the cream of the crop that Hungary lost to the west, and his story is one which must be preserved through the years.

Swimming Across is Grove's story which can be found on Amazon. I strongly urge you to read his story.

A Hungarian-born American businessman, engineer, author, and a science pioneer in the semiconductor industry. He escaped from Communist-controlled Hungary at the age of 20 and moved to the United States where he finished his education. He was one of the founders and the CEO of Intel Corporation, helping transform the company into the world's largest manufacturer of semiconductors.

When he was eight, the Nazis occupied Hungary and deported nearly 500,000 Jews to concentration camps, including Auschwitz. Its commandant, Rudolf Höss, said at his trial that he killed 400,000 Hungarian Jews in three months. To avoid being arrested, Grove and his mother took on false identities and were sheltered by friends. His father, however, was arrested and taken to an Eastern Labor Camp to do forced labor and was reunited with his family after the war.

During the Hungarian Revolution of 1956, when he was 20, he left his home and family and escaped across the border into Austria. Penniless and barely able to speak English, in 1957 he eventually made his way to the United States. He later changed his name to the anglicized, Andrew S. Grove. Grove summarized his first twenty years of life in Hungary in his memoirs:

"By the time I was twenty, I had lived through a Hungarian Fascist dictatorship, German military occupation, the Nazis' "Final Solution," the siege of Budapest by the Soviet Red Army, a period of chaotic democracy in the years immediately after the war, a variety of repressive Communist regimes, and a popular uprising that was put down at gunpoint where many young people were killed and countless others were interned. Some two hundred thousand Hungarians escaped to the West. I was one of them."

I've read Mr. Grove's story "Swimming Across" and like the others it is compelling and repeats the common experiences of these young boys and men through World War II, the Nazi occupation and holocaust remembrances (Grove was a Jew), the brutal Communist years culminating in the 1956 revolution and Russian occupation.

A part of Andy Grove's story that stands out is the reception he received upon arrival in the United States. At every turn, it seems, Grove was kindly treated and helped in many small and large ways. Like finding a relative and housing in New York City. He was outfitted with new clothing replacing the clothes he wore for over a month during his escape from Hungary to a brief settlement in Vienna Austria, to a long train ride to Germany followed by a two week long ocean voyage to Brooklyn New York.

Grove had completed a fair amount of university education in chemistry while in Hungary, and in seeking to complete his goal of becoming a chemist, he was helped along the way to becoming a chemical engineer with interviews and scholarship aid at several New York schools.

And of course it is widely known that Andrew Grove was one of the small group of founders of Intel Corporation, and was its CEO for many years. (Source –Wikipedia)

Read now what Andy Grove says about his life in America:

"I have loved my life in the United States. The doors that the International Rescue Committee and Professor Schmidt opened for me were just the first of many. I went through graduate school on scholarships, got a fantastic job at Fairchild Semiconductor, the high-flying company of its day, then participated in the founding of Intel, which in time has become the largest maker of semiconductors in the world. I rose to be its chief executive officer, a position I held for eleven years, until I stepped down from it in 1998; I continue as chairman today. I've continued to be amazed by the fact that as I progressed

through school and my career, no one has ever resented my success on account of my being an immigrant."

I was born in Budapest, Hungary, in 1936. By the time I was twenty, I had lived through a Hungarian Fascist dictatorship, German military occupation, the Nazis' "Final Solution," the siege of Budapest by the Soviet Red Army, a period of chaotic democracy in the years immediately after the war, a variety of repressive Communist regimes, and a popular uprising that was put down at gunpoint.

This is the story of that time and what happened to my family and me.

Before I tell my story, it may be helpful to provide some historical context. When I was born, Hungary was governed by the right-wing dictatorship of Admiral Miklos Horthy. Horthy's government was aligned with Nazi Germany, but it was more independent than Nazi Germany's other allies. This may have had something to do with the fact that Hungary was situated between the countries under Germany's influence and the Soviet Union.

During the early years of World War II, Hungary maintained a policy of armed neutrality. However, when Hitler's Germany attacked the Soviet Union in June 1941, Hungary abandoned that policy and declared war against the Allies. For all intents and purposes, this meant declaring war against the Soviet Union on the side of Nazi Germany.

By 1943, the Soviet army had the Germans and their Hungarian allies in retreat, and the front began to work its way through Hungary from its eastern borders toward the capital, Budapest. The Germans were concerned that

Horthy might try to negotiate a separate peace with the advancing Russians. To preempt that possibility, they occupied Hungary in March 1944 and, in October, installed an extreme Fascist government under the pro-Nazi Arrow Cross Party.

While the Horthy regime had discriminated against Hungarian Jews, the severity of the discrimination and persecution skyrocketed with the arrival of the Germans. Gestapo official Adolf Eichmann, who oversaw the implementation of the Nazis' Final Solution throughout the rest of Europe, took personal charge of the deportation and extermination of Hungarian Jews. The extermination process started in the countryside and the cities outside of Budapest; within four months, virtually all Hungarian Jews living outside of Budapest had been deported. The great majority of them were killed in concentration camps.

Before the process could be extended to Budapest, the rapidly deteriorating military situation — the Soviet forces were advancing on Budapest, and the Western Allies had successfully landed in Normandy and Italy — forced a halt to the deportations. Consequently, the majority of Jews in Budapest survived. Nevertheless, before the war, there were over six hundred fifty thousand Jews living in Hungary; after the war, some one hundred fifty thousand remained.

In January 1945, after street-to-street and house-to-house fighting, the Soviet army pushed the Germans out of Budapest and, by April, out of the rest of Hungary as well. Instead of a German occupation army, there was now a Soviet occupation army.

In the immediate aftermath of the war, despite the presence of the Soviet occupying forces, Hungary enjoyed a multiparty democracy. However, the Communist Party gained more and more influence and finally consolidated its position in 1948. Thereafter, Hungary became an unquestioned satellite of the Soviet Union.

The Hungarian Communist Party was divided into two major branches: the native Hungarian Communist branch, which had remained in Hungary even after the Communist Party in Hungary was outlawed by the Horthy regime; and the Muscovite branch, whose members had escaped to the Soviet Union and had now returned with the Russian troops. Matyas Rakosi was the preeminent leader of the Muscovite branch. Although both branches belonged to the same political party, there was a degree of distrust between them that grew as they jockeyed for positions of authority in the Communist regime.

By 1949, this jockeying for position broke into the open with the arrest and public trial of native Hungarian Communists by the Muscovites. The persecution intensified during the last few years of the life of the leader of the Soviet Union, Joseph Stalin, with purges, arrests, imprisonment, and deportation affecting the lives of broader and broader circles of people.

Stalin died in March 1953, and a gradual relaxation of totalitarian controls took place. Over the next few years, this process accelerated until it culminated in a rebellion against the Communist government — the Hungarian revolution of October 1956.

The revolt lasted for thirteen days and was then put down by Soviet armed forces. Many young people were killed; countless others were interned. Some two hundred thousand Hungarians escaped to the West.

I was one of them.

From Starvation in Ukraine to Success in Montana

Martel family in 1943, about one year before they started their historic trek.

Our home for several years now is Helena Montana. We settled here, just an hour's drive to Butte where Diana and I were raised. It seems we are not the only "immigrants" coming into Montana these days as an article I read about recent Bozeman 'immigration' outlined.

I read the article yesterday as I was finishing the story of a family that immigrated to Bozeman in 1953 - the Martel family. Their story is told in the book *"The Last Green Valley"* A Novel at:

https://www.amazon.com/Last-Green-Valley-Mark-Sullivan-ebook/dp/B07CGCTSNW/ref=sr_1_1?crid=39MLJXP19I5C3&dchild=1&keywords=the+last+green+valley+mark+sullivan&qid=1620910967&sprefix=the+last+green+valley%2Caps%2C260&sr=8-1

Author Mark Sullivan is also from Bozeman.

In short, the Martel family came to the US from Ukraine the hard way – a very hard way. At the end of WW-II they were expelled from their home close to the Russian border by the Russians. The Martels' were ethnic German and found themselves on an incredibly arduous exit to Germany escorted by the retreating German army following their defeat by the Red Army. They were very close to making it to the Allied lines in Germany when Emil was arrested by Romanian soldiers and sent off to a forced labor camp in Ukraine.

He eventually escaped and made his way to the British sector of Berlin. His wife Adeline also managed to escape to the British sector where she and the two boys reunited with Emil.

They wound up in Bozeman as refugees, where Adeline discovered *The Last Green Valley* of her dreams. Here's how Adeline described the dream she held onto during her journey from tyranny to liberty.

"Tell me again, Mama, about where we're going." "It's a beautiful place," Adeline whispered sleepily. "It's surrounded by mountains and forests. And snow up high. And below there will be a winding river and green fields. We will live in a warm home, and every morning I will bake bread for you, and there will be a big garden in the back, and we'll have so much food, we won't know what to do with it all."

The arrival in New York Harbor …

By then, the fog had blown away to the east, revealing the lady in all her glory. Emil stared up at the statue in awe, shook his fist, and whispered, "Freedom. All a man could ever want." "We still have to find Mama's green valley," Will said.

This was a very difficult story to read, but I knew the end would be quite different and inspirational – it was! When I finally got to that place in the story where they arrived at *The Last Green Valley*, the tears began to flow. Here's how the author put it - -

"This is an American story, an immigrant story, a spiritual and universal story. May we all dare to chase such dreams, experience such grace, and lead such miraculous lives."
       —Mark Sullivan, Bozeman, Montana, July 21, 2020

From that very humble and tenuous beginning, the Martel family started and grew what has become the premier construction company in the state of Montana. Take a look at Martel Construction Bozeman/Bigfork/Missoula

https://www.martelconstruction.com/

The Martel legacy:

Martel Construction is Montana's premier general contracting firm.

I'm drawn to such stories of people who have come to that 'Shining City On A Hill,' often from horrific places of tyranny and war such as the Soviet Union and Nazi Germany. I have known some of them.

Read the PREFACE by the author to get a flavor of the story, the Martel family and their journey to freedom and opportunity.

PREFACE People told me I would never find another untold World War II story like that of Pino Lella, the hero and basis of my historical novel Beneath a Scarlet Sky. I honestly believed I would, however, and paid close attention to the dozens of letters and pitches I received from people telling me other stories from that time period. They were all wonderfully interesting in their way. But none of them matched my criteria, which were that the underlying tale had to be inherently moving, inspiring, and potentially transformative to me and so to readers. Then, in November 2017, I was asked to speak about Pino to the noontime Rotary Club in my hometown of Bozeman, Montana. A retired dentist came up to me afterward to outline a story a local man had told him. It caught my attention immediately. Two days later, I put the man's address in my GPS and saw it was less than two miles from my own . The closer I got, I felt odd, and I had no idea why. It wasn't until I pulled into his driveway and got out of my car that I realized I was no more than two hundred yards away from the home where I'd first heard Pino Lella's story nearly eleven years before. That story changed my life. I went to the door, knocked, and my life changed again.

Within fifteen minutes of listening to the particulars of the story of the Martel family, I was more than interested. By the end of two hours, I believed I had a tale to tell that would be a worthy successor to the tale that inspired Beneath. And I'd heard it in the same little neighborhood where I'd first heard Pino's story. What were the odds of that? For the next fifteen months after that first meeting, I interviewed survivors and researched and traveled to critical locations in the story, including the ruins of an abandoned farmhouse in deeply rural, far - western Ukraine. From there, I retraced the dangerous and remarkable journey of a young family of refugees on the run westward in a wagon with two horses, often caught between the retreating German armies and the advancing Soviets in the final chaotic year of World War II .

I trailed the Martels' route through present - day Moldova, Romania, Hungary, the Czech Republic, and Poland, where the way split: one continuing west and another doubling back east more than eleven hundred miles to the former site of a deadly Soviet POW camp set in the bleak postwar rubble near the Ukrainian border with Belarus. Along the way, I interviewed participants and eyewitnesses to the "Long Trek" as well as Holocaust, military, and refugee historians, who helped me to understand the context in which the Martels' story unfolded and why. I also listened to the recordings of people, long dead, describing the ordeal and felt in awe of the grit, humanity, and spirit they showed in the face of seemingly insurmountable challenges and odds. Even though I had all that information and understanding when I sat down to write this book, there were holes in the tale not completely explained by the limited material I had to rely on. To bridge those gaps, I have been forced to draw on my own suspicions and imagination to bring the story more fully to life. What you are about to read, then, is not narrative nonfiction, but historical fiction based on an extraordinary tale of World War II and its aftermath. As I am finishing this novel, the world is engulfed in the crisis of a century, and the way forward seems as dangerous and unclear as it must have been for the Martels when they set out on their journey. It is my dream that their story will give comfort and courage to the afflicted and a better understanding of what ordinary people can endure and achieve even when all seems lost.

Bill and Walter Martel [the children] overcome with emotion after finding the ruins of their childhood home in Friedenstahl.

I finally had the pleasure of meeting with Bill Martel. It was a very enjoyable time of learning and getting acquainted with a remarkable man and his story. Here is my report from that get together:

The story is of their forced Long Trek out of Ukraine through Moldova, Romania, the Czech Republic, and Poland. And finally post war divided Germany. See the map below.

I came across this book through advertising on the internet. I noticed that the author and the subjects of the book were Montanans from Bozeman, so I purchased the book and then added a summary of it to this book on immigration.

The setting was Eastern Europe in 1945, the final year of the war (see map below). The family was forced from their home by the Soviets and were looking and yearning for peace and freedom to the west. Germany was being defeated by the Allied powers, including the Soviet Union from which they had just been forcibly expelled.

Much of the book is very detailed, with many of those details provided by Bill and some conversations of his father Emil secretly recorded over time.

I listened intently as Bill recalled much of what I had read several times in Sullivan's book. Bill's detailed memory from his childhood at age 8-12 reminded me of the detailed recollections of my friend and Navy shipmate Adam von Dioszeghy during his war-time childhood experiences of World War-II Budapest, the communist years that followed, and his part in the 1956 Hungarian Revolution.

Bill has vivid memories of them being caught in a tank battle between the retreating German army and the

Soviet Red Army. He also recalled his father whipping the two horses in a desperate attempt to escape the battle. And more ...

As the family neared Berlin and the hoped-for freedom in the West, Emil was arrested and sent back deep into Ukraine to a forced labor camp. This was a death camp with much disease, hard labor and very little food. Bill said that around 10 dead bodies were hauled away every day. The 600 captives when he first arrived had dwindled down to 200. Emil feared he was soon to be next and made a desperate and successful escape.

Bill's personal recollections of these events are vivid, and obviously etched deeply in his very being. He and his brother Walt, along with Mark Sullivan made a recent trip back to Ukraine and visited the old Martel home near Odessa, and also the forced labor camp near Poltava Ukraine. See the picture below and follow the link to learn more of this camp and the area of the prison camp.

Life in the forced labor camp. See: poltava prison camp ukraine - Bing

Being in the very camp where their father suffered was very emotional for Bill and Walt, and I could see that in Bill's face and heard it in his voice as he recalled the visit.

Life in Ukraine has long been brutal and deadly. We see and hear much in today's news about the Russian invasion of Ukraine and the ongoing war there. The current war and the situation in today's Ukraine did not come up in my visit with Bill Martel, but I'm sure it must weigh on his mind. But Bill, in several of his remarks, and as his lifetime as an American show, is very much a proud and grateful American.

Take a look at this article, The Holocaust in Ukraine – Wikipedia to learn of the Holocaust in Ukraine when millions of Jews perished under the Nazi program of genocide against the Jews. Earlier, in the early 1930s, the communists under Joseph Stalin instituted the Holodomor where millions of Ukrainians died of forced starvation. Read more at Holodomor – Wikipedia.

Bill describes his life as a life filled with miracles. One of these miracles was the reuniting of the family. Following the war millions of people were displaced and scattered everywhere. There were no computers, no internet, just such things as Red Cross bulletin boards, and eventually newspapers where many posted inquiries searching for loved ones. And yet, the Martel family was reunited in West Germany through the Red Cross.

Another miracle of this family reunion was the escape of Adeline and the two boys. Adeline and the boys were in the eastern Soviet area of Germany and Emil was in the western area. The Soviets had closed the border down tight in either direction. Getting across was very perilous, and many died at the hands of the Soviets during attempted border crossings.

Another miracle was finding a sponsor in small town Baker Montana. Thus began a shift in Bill's story towards assimilation into America.

The picture below shows Bill sitting on a box in the Martel Construction company's headquarters in Bozeman.

This box contained all of the possessions of the Martel family when they arrived in Baker Montana. The box is a very important artifact for the family, and it vividly shows their remarkable assimilation into American life when contrasted with the remarkable growth and success of the Martel Construction company statewide in Montana – and beyond. I'll paraphrase one of Bill's remarks *"Only in American could all this have happened"* to which I responded, *"Your story Bill, is an exceptional story ... but one that is very common here."* Bill concurred with that. A quick look back at the book and I see his mother Adeline saying, *"Only in America is a story like ours possible."* As author Sullivan says" *Indeed, Adeline would live to see Bill driven to success by a small, empty, wooden packing crate he kept outside his office door."*

Click on the links below to see the remarkable work accomplished over the years from their humble beginnings of building and selling simple small homes in Bozeman. Bill told me a few stories of that growth.

Martel Construction – Bozeman I Bigfork I Missoula

https://www.martelconstruction.com/

And a bit of the company history:

History – martelconstruction https://www.martelconstruction.com/History

Here is Bill on the deck overlooking the back yard of his beautiful home in the hills of Bozeman. He told me of their first home in Bozeman where they finished off the basement and lived down there while building the rest of the house above. I can relate to this as I recalled my paper route in Butte where many also lived in basements while completing the home above. In those days, it was' cash and carry', or more accurately 'cash and build as you were able'.

Years ago, I did a PechaKucha presentation on *"Amazing and Interesting People I Have Known."*

Among them are: Sam Jankovich, Adam von Dioszeghy, Gene Beckstrom, Sam Thomas, Terry Wilcox, Jerry Beall, Dick emery, Sal & Renee Marini ....

And now I add Bill Martel to that still growing list.

I am grateful for each of these who have come personally into my life. They have made a difference.

Bill Martel understands liberty. Bill Martel understands and has lived where liberty does not exist. And Bill Martel understands that the America he grew up into is an exceptional nation. Bill Martel understands that exceptionalism is derived from the Constitutional twin pillars of Liberty and Opportunity.

At the end of our time together, Bill gave he a hard copy of the book. Notice Bill's tag line – *"Cherish your freedom"*.

I invite you to take a look at my own study and analysis of this precious thing called Liberty. And while you are there, take a look at my 3-book series "ON LIBERTY"

Amazon.com: Yearning for Liberty (ON LIBERTY): 9781983209222: Johnson, Donald L: Books

Finally, here is a map with the red lines showing the travels of the Martel family as they make their way west in 1945.

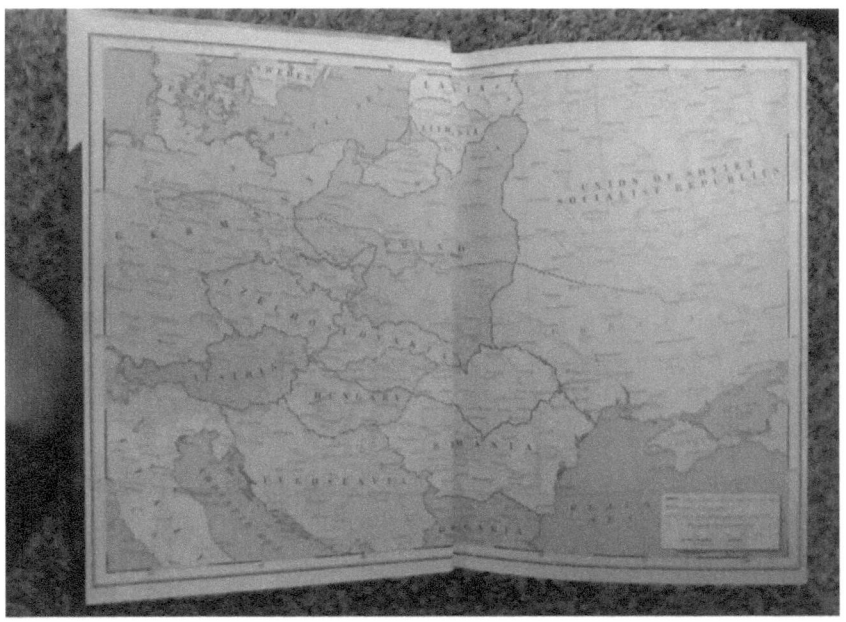

From Liberia -- Meet the Mayor of Helena Montana

I've been in Helena Montana since March 2, 2020 as the pandemic lock down extended our visit with an aunt. Aunt Jean has welcomed us into her home during this time and we are all happy to be together helping one another.

After being here for a while, I discovered the mayor of Helena – Wilmot Collins. Here was a black man in Montana, one of less than 1% in the entire state as well as in Helena, Hmmm. Amazing. How could this be?

My first blush reaction was positive, and pride welled up for the state of my birth and upbringing, but not my home since my late teens. I decided I would hold off in learning about this man and his story and let this unlikely happening percolate in my mind and soul. As I learn more about the mayor, I may not like him, but then again, like so many of the Helena voters that made him mayor, perhaps I will like him as well.

After several months of living in Helena we have decided to relocate here. It's a nice community of roughly 30,000 people and we have come to like it very much and seeing Mr. Collins as mayor has contributed to that feeling.

So let's take a look at our Mayor in his own words. *Source:* https://www.pri.org/stories/2016-05-25/what-he-ll-say-new-refugees-montana-i-will-tell-them-you-have-have-thick-skin (edited)

See also: **He Left a War-Torn Country as a Refugee and Went on to Become a US Mayor** https://ayearningforpublius.wordpress.com/2021/09/18/he-left-a-war-torn-country-as-a-refugee-and-went-on-to-become-a-us-mayor/

His message to new refugees in Montana: *'You have to have thick skin'*

Montana is one of two states that does not have an office to accept refugees. But that's about to change, and Wilmot Collins wants his new neighbors to know that they can make a life here. He spoke about his journey from Liberia at a meeting on April 22, 2016. His son, Bliss, sits at the table.

When Wilmot Collins and his wife Maddie arrived in Ghana after escaping the Liberian civil war in September 1990, he weighed just 90 pounds. Maddie was about 87 pounds. They were starving, dehydrated and sick. Both had to be rushed to the hospital.

Four years later, they arrived in Helena, Montana, where they were resettled as refugees. Now Wilmot Collins, 52, works for the Department of Health and Human Services. Maddie Collins is a registered nurse. They own their own home. Their 24-year-old daughter is in the Navy while their 20-year-old son, formerly a high school football star, is a sophomore at the University of Montana.

Collins wants people to hear his story because he wants them to know that new refugees have something to offer.

And new refugees are coming: Montana is one of two states without a refugee resettlement office, but the International Rescue Committee will open an office in Missoula this summer. (The other state is Wyoming.) The last time the IRC had an office in Montana was 25 years ago; it closed in 1991 after a push to resettle Hmong refugees fleeing Vietnam was completed.

With the Obama administration under a tight deadline to hit its goal of resettling 10,000 Syrian refugees before the end of the year, there is a good chance some Syrian families may be among the first 25 or so refugees headed to Missoula.

Collins wants these new arrivals to know that whatever initial difficulties they encounter, the state is a fundamentally a welcoming place.

Wilmot and Maddie Collins came to Montana in the 90s. At a *Soft Landing Missoula* event on April 22, he told his story of escaping Liberia. "My wife said, 'Let's go to Montana.' I said, 'Where is that?'

Collins has encountered both sides of that coin. When he first arrived to Montana in 1994, the community had already rallied around his wife, who arrived more than two years earlier. He got off the plane to find a welcoming party put together by students at Helena High School and members of The First Lutheran Church. They held sheets of paper that together spelled out "Welcome home Wilmot."

"We got to the airport, man, it was like a foreign dignitary visiting Montana. And I'm like, all this for me? This refugee from Liberia?"

Eight weeks later, he got a call from a neighbor with news he didn't expect. Word had gotten around town about the new refugee from Africa — and not everyone was so welcoming. His neighbor told him that someone tried to set his car on fire and wrote in black letters, "Go back to Africa" and "KKK" on the white siding of his home.

Collins was shocked and his wife was worried. He called the police and met them at their home. But by the time they got there to survey the damage, the neighbors had already started washing it off.

"When I saw that, I was shocked because I had never experienced that before and I didn't know what to make of it. But when I started processing what went on, I said,

'Wow, the outcome is good. My neighbors are good people.'"

"I think the people of Montana are very accepting and welcoming," Collins says, reflecting on the incident. "But the problems we have is that without information, we tend to stick to what we hear. That is, if we do not educate the public on what refugees are about, they will stick to whatever bigotry they hear."

"That's why they tried burning my car," he says. "That's why the marked my home 'KKK,' 'Go back to Africa' — because they didn't know me. Today, I don't think they can say that. I know in my own small way, I've enriched the community. Talk to my students, talk to my former students, talk to my military mates, talk to my co-workers."

For Maddie and Wilmot Collins, coming to the US wasn't easy. In their first few months in Montana, their home was graffitied with "Go back to Africa" and "KKK." But they stayed.

"Education is the key. People will hear things and not research. I went through that process. I went through the bigotry, I went through the racism, and in the end I stayed here. That means something. There are good people here. I think the Syrian refugees will be accepted, but with every initial crisis, there will be a lot of negativity going on. We just have to stand firm and tell the truth," Collins says.

And part of that truth is found in his experience.

"The only thing they're looking for is a second chance at life. Believe me, I was dying of starvation. The US gave me a second chance. I will never abuse it. "

About eight months ago, Collins met a Cuban refugee couple, Adonis Antolin and Maie Lee Jones, who had moved to Helena with their two young daughters. Helena is not a diverse town by any measure — according to the 2010 census, it's 93 percent white and 0.6 percent African American. Antolin is Afro-Cuban and told Collins he was worried about how he and his family would fit in.

"He told us to be patient because here, it's different. There aren't that many Latino people or black people. He told me not to feel scared because people here are very nice," Antolin says.

Collins also helped the family get access to basic services while they got on their feet and gave them advice on things like where to get the best food. Now, Antolin works as a maintenance worker for a nonprofit while Lee Jones works in data entry. They are glad they stayed.

"We were thinking of going to Miami, but he was one of the people who told us to stay. He said Helena was a good place to raise a family. Thanks to him, I'm here, really," Antolin says.

Antolin's change of heart didn't surprise Collins.

"I've been here 22 years. I've never once thought about leaving. It says a lot," Collins says. "I came here speaking English, so what about the refugees that are coming from Syria that are Muslim? I think they will experience some racism, I think they will experience some bigotry, but all in all, at the end of the day, I think there will be acceptance."

Other Collins references:

https://www.carnegie.org/awards/honoree/wilmot-collins/

https://www.npr.org/2019/10/09/767275774/in-montana-a-liberian-refugee-mounts-u-s-senate-challenge

Those who follow this author's blog and read some of my books will see that I value immigrant Americans such as Wilmot Collins. I have been especially drawn in with the stories of refugees from the 1956 Hungarian Revolution, and in particular my dear friend and Navy Shipmate Adam von Dioszeghy. I can now add Mayor Wilmot Collins to my growing list of valued American citizens. And I notice that many of these have been refugees from horrific violence and upheaval around the world, thus ingraining in them a very personal love and respect of liberty, and gratitude towards their new nation.

The Mayor Collins story is but one of many that puts the lie to the prevailing Marxist Critical Race Theory that seeks to divide people into two classes – Racist White Supremacists vs. People of Color. We are seeing the destructive consequences of that theory being played out nationwide in this spring and summer of 2020.

From Cuba (one among many)

I came across this man as he spoke at the 2020 Republican National Convention. Immediately I found his life story to be a fit for inclusion into the Hungarian model.

Listen to his story.

"My name is Maximo Alvarez. I'm speaking to you today from my home in South Florida -not far from the Straits of Florida which isn't just a 90-mile wide blue strip on a map for me. It divides freedom from fear. It divides the past from the future.

I know all about the past -I'll never forget my own. My family has fled totalitarianism and communism. And more than once. First from Spain, then from Cuba.

But my family is done leaving. By the grace of God, I have lived the American dream—the greatest blessing I've ever had. My dad, who only had a sixth-grade education told me, "don't lose this place. You'll never be as lucky as me."

I'm speaking to you today because my family is done leaving places. **There is nowhere left to go.**

I'm speaking to you today because President Trump may not always care about being polite —-but all the far left cares about is power. Power for them - not for us.

I'm speaking to you today because I've seen people like this before. I've seen movements like this before. I've seen ideas like this before and I'm here to tell you, we cannot let them take over our country.

I heard the promises of Fidel Castro. And I can never forget all those who grew up around me, who looked like me, who could have been me, who suffered and starved and died because they believed those empty promises.

Go to Freedom Tower in Miami. Stop to listen and you can still hear the sound of those promises being broken. It is the sound of waves in the ocean, carrying families clinging to pieces of wood, families with children who can't swim, but willing to risk everything to reach this blessed land. It is the sound of tears hitting the paper of an application for American citizenship.

They heard the empty promises and they know the reality. Look at them. Listen to them. Learn the truth. Those false promises - spread the wealth, defund the police, trust a socialist state more than your family and community— don't sound radical to my ears. They sound familiar.

When Fidel Castro was asked if he was a communist, he said he was a Roman Catholic. He knew he had to hide the truth. But the country I was born in is gone — destroyed. When I watch the news in Seattle and Chicago and Portland, when I see history being rewritten, when I hear the promises — I hear echoes of a former life I never wanted to hear again. I see shadows I thought I had outrun.

My parents only wanted one person to decide my fate — me. Not some party member, not some government official, not some bureaucrat — in America, I would decide my own future.

I am so grateful to America, the place where I was able to build my American dream through hard work and determination. President Trump knows that the American story was written by people just like you and me, who love our country and take risks to build a future for our families and neighbors.

I may be Cuban born, but I am 100 percent American. This is the greatest country in the world. If I gave away everything I have today, it would not equal 1 percent of what I was given when I came to this great country: The gift of Freedom.

Right now – It is up to us to decide our fate and to choose freedom over oppression.

President Trump is fighting against the forces of socialism, communism, and totalitarianism. And he will continue to do just that. And what about his opponent and the rest of the DC swamp? I have no doubt they will hand the country over to those dangerous forces.

You and I will decide. And here is what I've decided: I choose President Trump because I choose America."

Cuban family celebrates 61 years of freedom in America.

I escaped Castro's Cuba for freedom in America. Sixty-one years later my family still celebrates our arrival | Fox News

September 3 is a very special day for my family. What happened on this date in 1962 is etched on hearts forever

This 3rd day of September will be a very special anniversary for the Sanchez family. As we will celebrate our 61st year in the United States, for the Sanchez family it is a celebration of living in freedom in the greatest country ever created.

September 3, 1962, holds a special meaning for my family; it is a day my mother, brothers and I will never forget. It is the date my mom, two older brothers and I left behind the tyranny of Castro's Socialist Cuba to come to the freedom of the United States. This year marks the 61st anniversary of that day.

My father fled Cuba in 1961 on a cargo ship bound for Spain to escape communists who were after him.

My mother stayed behind with me and my two older brothers, Juan, who at 10 years old was now the man of the house, and Guillermo, age 9, in the house that she and my father had built in the suburbs of Havana. Goons from Cuba's revolutionary army would come by at all times of the day and night to harass my mom.

They would call her names and shout at her that she would lose her home soon and that we were traitors to the communist revolution. My two older brothers were always at my mom's side when the soldiers came, helping her and standing strong with her.

My parents taught me that freedom is something you never take for granted, you cherish it, you fight for it and you share it.

When Castro closed all the country's Catholic schools, my mom pulled my two brothers from the public schools. My mom did not want her sons to attend public schools where the children were being indoctrinated by the communists to believe in Fidel as the Supreme Being and that there was no God.

My father, who stayed in Spain for just a few months after his arrival, was eventually granted political asylum in the United States and immediately began the paperwork to have us leave on one of the Freedom Flights President Kennedy had arranged for Cuban families seeking freedom in the United States.

Waiting to be reunited

As a young boy, I would often ask my mother where papa was. She always replied that I would see him again soon, but he was always close in my heart. Not long after my father began to work on having our family removed from Cuba, my mother — who told me this story — finally received the good news that she would be able to leave Cuba with her three sons.

For many months she had fought with Cuba's communist government to allow Juan, my eldest brother, to leave the country with us. (The Cuban government wanted Juan to stay behind since he was 10 years old and could soon begin military training and communist indoctrination.) My mom won — she is one tough lady when she has to be.

Today she is 92 and loves America with all her heart. When I awoke the morning of Sept. 3, 1962, I had no idea what would happen to my family and me on that day.

My mom grabbed a few family photographs, a dress and one set of clothing for each of her three boys and stuffed everything into one small suitcase.

The communist government did not allow us to leave with any possessions such as money, jewelry or anything else, just that one small suitcase for four people.

That day was one of mixed emotions for my mother. On the one hand, she wanted to rejoin her husband in the United States so her three children could be raised in freedom. Cuba had become a nation without freedom of religion or speech and a land of tyranny.

On the other hand, she would leave her home, the land she loved and had never expected to leave. She would also be leaving behind her aging parents and her brothers and sisters, not knowing if she would ever see them again.

On that morning, my mom, my brothers and I went outside our house so that Pepe, a family friend, could take us to the airport for the 1:00 p.m. Cubana Airlines flight to Miami. As my grandparents hugged and kissed us, my mom hugged her father, mother, brothers and sisters for what would be the last time in her life — I cannot even imagine this experience, can you?

As we sat in the back seat of the car, my mom turned in her seat to look through the back window to wave goodbye to her parents, family members and friends. After being searched by Cuban soldiers, we boarded the plane and were on our way to freedom. One of the few things I do remember was seeing the ground below as the airplane took off.

Arrival in the United States

We arrived in Miami before 2:00 p.m. and were immediately taken to immigration processing at the Freedom Tower (the old Miami News building on Biscayne Boulevard) where we received our medical shots, a toothbrush and toothpaste. The U.S. government placed us at the Tamiami Hotel in downtown Miami for the next two nights.

On Sept. 5, we took a flight to New York City to rejoin our father. When we got off the plane at LaGuardia, my father was waiting. He hugged my mom, brothers and me so hard while crying.

Years later, my brother Juan told me that was the first time he had ever seen our papa cry. Our family had been reunited in freedom.

Living in freedom

Less than 30 days after we arrived in the United States, the Cuban Missile Crisis began and all Freedom Flights from Cuba were canceled.

Although my family never thought, nor even desired to leave Cuba, my parents accepted political asylum in this great country and were always grateful that America opened her arms to them.

My father had, and my mom continues to have, a deep love for the United States. They never protested against any policy of this country and they always obeyed her laws.

They viewed themselves as guests during the early years following our arrival, but after years passed, and the possibility of returning to their beloved Cuba faded, they proudly became citizens of America. Years later I would serve in our military to say thank you to America.

My parents never accepted any form of welfare or aid; they both worked in the most menial jobs you can imagine, around the clock, to provide for their children.

My mom was a housewife in Cuba, but here she worked in a factory making plastic coolers and bags in the Bronx.

My father started working at Incarnation Catholic Church in Manhattan as a maintenance man and worked at Merrill Lynch at night cleaning offices.

They never complained or asked, "Why me?" We had a comfortable middle-class lifestyle in Cuba before it all crumbled as Castro's communist revolution seized all private property.

My parents taught me that freedom is something you never take for granted, you cherish it, you fight for it and you share it.

If I ever have a "bad hair day," the mere thought of my parents' experience puts things back into perspective.

I cannot even begin to tell you how grateful I am to my parents and to this great country, the United States and look forward to celebrating this special anniversary for our family.

From Communist China

Again, during the 2020 Republican National Convention I heard this man's story. Again, a good fit into the model.

Here is his story.

During the third night of the 2020 RNC convention, Chinese dissident and civil rights attorney Chen Guangcheng, who has been blind since childhood, conducted his speech by reading braille and speaking in his second language. He warned about the evils of the Chinese Communist Party [CCP] after experiencing their tyranny firsthand.

"Standing up to tyranny is not easy. I know. When I spoke out against China's 'one child' policy and other injustices, I was persecuted, beaten, and put under house arrest by the government. In April, 2012, I escaped and was given shelter in the American embassy in Beijing. I am forever grateful to the American people for welcoming me and my family to the United States where we are now free," Guangcheng said. "The Chinese Communist Party is an enemy of humanity. It is terrorizing its own people and it is threatening the well-being of the world. In China, expressing beliefs or ideas not approved by the CCP - religion, democracy, human rights - can lead to prison. The nation lives under mass surveillance and censorship. The CCP is focused on power and control, and acts without regard to the law or to human rights. Countless activists have disappeared or are under house arrest. Just consider the sad plight of the Uyghurs in concentration camps."

Guangcheng also discussed the CCP's latest assault on the world.

"The coronavirus pandemic, originating in China—and covered up by the CCP—has caused mass death and social upheaval around the world. In the same way, the virus of the CCP is threatening the people of the world. The policy of appeasement of former administrations—including Obama and Biden—has allowed the CCP to infiltrate and corrode different aspects of the global community," he said.

The US must use its values of freedom, democracy, and the rule of law, to gather a coalition of other democracies to stop China's aggression. President Trump has led on this and we need the other countries to join him in this fight. A fight for our future," Guengcheng continued.

From the Communist Chinese Cultural Revolution

[Sight, a Film Based on the True Story of World-Famous Eye Surgeon Ming Wang, Releases May 24 - The Stream](#)

Diana and I watched this film recently, a very moving and touching story of a young man's story of realizing a boyhood dream of becoming a doctor. The fulfillment of a dream made possible because of the liberty he found in America, liberty that provided Wing Wang the freedom and opportunity to achieve his dream.

And, in the fulfillment of that dream, Dr. Wang blessed countless others with the gift of vision.

I encourage all to learn of this remarkable story.

Read more of this remarkable story at:

https://fromdarknesstosight.com/

From Darkness to Sight shares the remarkable life journey of Dr. Ming Wang, a world-renowned laser eye surgeon and philanthropist. It is an inspirational story of how one man turned fear, poverty, persecution, and prejudice into healing and love for others.

As a teenager, Ming fought valiantly to escape one of history's darkest eras— China's Cultural Revolution—during which millions of innocent youth were deported to remote areas to face a life sentence of poverty and hard labor. Through his own tenacity and his parents' tireless efforts to provide a chance of freedom for their son, Ming eventually made his way to America with only $50 and a Chinese-English dictionary in his pocket, but with an American dream in his heart. Against all odds, he earned a PhD in laser physics and graduated magna cum laude with the highest honors from Harvard Medical School and MIT. He embraced the Christian faith and tackled one of the most important questions of our time — are faith and science friends or foes? — which led to his invention of a breakthrough biotechnology to restore sight.

Dr. Wang has performed over 55,000 eye procedures on patients from nearly every state in the U.S. and over 55 countries. These include over 4,000 physicians, earning him the moniker "the doctors' doctor." He received the Outstanding Nashvillian of the Year Award from Kiwanis Club International, NPR's Philanthropist of the Year Award and an honorary doctorate degree from Trevecca Nazarene University.

Dr. Wang has published eight textbooks and over 100 articles, including one in the world-renowned journal Nature, holds several U.S. patents, and performed the world's first laser-assisted artificial cornea implantation. He received the Honor

Award from the American Academy of Ophthalmology and the Lifetime Achievement Award from the Association of Chinese American Physicians.

Dr. Wang is currently the only surgeon in the state [Tennessee] who performs 3D LASIK (18+), 3D FOREVER YOUNG™ lens surgery (45+), and 3D Laser Cataract Surgery (60+). He established a non-profit foundation that provides sight restoration surgeries free of charge for indigent patients who otherwise would never be able to afford them.

From Congo – In Helena Montana

(This article from Helena Area Refugee Resettlement Team. Emphasis is mine)

We in Helena, Montana, have recently welcomed a wonderful refugee family from the DRC (Democratic Republic of Congo). They are the Lwamba family of 10: Grandmother, husband and wife, and 7 lovely children ranging from 17-2 years. Mama Lwamba is pregnant with her 8th child. These children are beautiful. The 7-year-old was hospitalized recently with seizures and high fever. Turns out he has residual malaria and faces a long regime of medications.

In 1999, they escaped the violence and civil war in the DRC, seeking refuge at the Nyarugusu refugee camp in Tanzania. They remained there for 25 years. All of their children were born in this camp.

This camp houses over 150,000 refugees. Residents of the camp are not permitted to leave. Imagine being confined to a camp for 25 years.

After so many years of waiting, **the family was vetted and approved to migrate to the USA. They are on a full path to citizenship.**

They are excited and overwhelmed starting this new life here in Montana. Everything is new and different. Papa Lwamba and the 17-year-old son taught themselves some English while at the camp and have conversational skills. Grandmother, Mama Lwamba, and the younger 6 kids only speak Swahili. This is just one of the challenges they face.

So many new experiences like the washing machine, the microwave, drinkable water from a faucet, and cooking on an electric stove (they used a clay and wood fire stove).

Due to their long stay in the camp and the lack of educational opportunities, they have minimal job skills. Papa Lwamba had wanted to be a teacher and had started his education before leaving the DRC. He is bright, thoughtful, and curious. He has just landed a job at a food service company. And here is the dilemma: He will not make enough money to support his family. They are housed in temporary housing costing $4000 per month, hopefully soon to be moved to a house costing $2500 plus utilities.

Grandmother is seeking a job and Mama Lwamba will work after her baby is born.

Their lives were so disadvantaged in the camp. Now they have been given a chance in a new country. They are committed to meeting the challenges but really do need financial assistance to become productive, integrated members of American society.

The kids are in school and the parents are so happy to have their children get an education.

Note from this author:

Note that the current mayor of Helana and his wife are also refugees from turmoil in Africa. Their story is here at "From Liberia … "

From Congo - New Haven Remembers Semi Semi-Dikoko

Semi-Semi Dikoko with David Sepulveda and Aleta Staton at the Arts Awards in December 2012. Judy Sirota Rosenthal Photo with permission from the Arts Council of Greater New Haven.

Author's note: We lived in this Westville neighborhood of New Haven for 11 years and knew Semi Semi-Dikoko. His story is remarkable as you will see in this wonderful article about Semi's life, it fits very nicely into the theme of this book. I hope you enjoy his story nicely written by Lucy Gellman of the Arts Council of Greater New Haven.

Maybe he offered you a glass of red wine as he floated through the studio, and pulled you into an embrace. Maybe you tended the apple trees together at Edgewood Park, or listened to poetry in the warm half-light of Lyric

Hall. Maybe you saw the beret across a crowded room, and knew that for a moment, all was well with the world.

His door was always open. He almost certainly called you *darling*, with a rolling *h* that you could reach out and touch. He may have pushed you to dream bigger than you thought possible. If you were lucky, you shared a tango and a tray of Brussels sprouts with him.

Semi Semi-Dikoko, a tireless advocate for the arts who blessed New Haven with three decades of a gentle and generous spirit, died at Smilow Cancer Hospital last Thursday, with the artist Amie Ziner at his side. The cause was prostate cancer, which Semi-Dikoko had been fighting bravely and often quietly for four years. In the past decade, he also battled lymphoma, which was until recently in remission. He was 69 years old.

He leaves behind his younger sisters, Annie Gumba and Lucienne Nkebani of New Haven, an older brother, Maxime Luzolo of Congo, nieces and cousins who adored him, and hundreds of New Haveners who are still reeling from his death. In over a dozen interviews, friends, family members, and colleagues remembered him as a brilliant and familiar presence, who always wanted to know what more he could do for the community.

"Semi just touched so many lives," said his friend and studio mate David Sepulveda. The two, who shared a studio at West River Arts, were so close they often seemed like two halves of the same, vibrantly beating heart.

He was trained as a systems architect and consultant, who worked for IBM, Fujitsu Americas, Deutsche Bank, NASA, and Southern New England Telecommunications (SNET) among others. He was a dedicated public servant, whose thousands of volunteer hours spanned

Friends of Edgewood Park to Artspace New Haven to the Westville Village Renaissance Alliance.

For most of his friends, he was Semi, a warm and constant presence who always had time for the people in his life.

"His art was human connectivity," said Aaron Goode, who met him over a decade ago when the two enrolled in the city's first Democracy School class. "That was his medium. He was a painter of civic canvases. Westville, that was one of his canvases, but so was New Haven and so was New York."

Curious & Calm

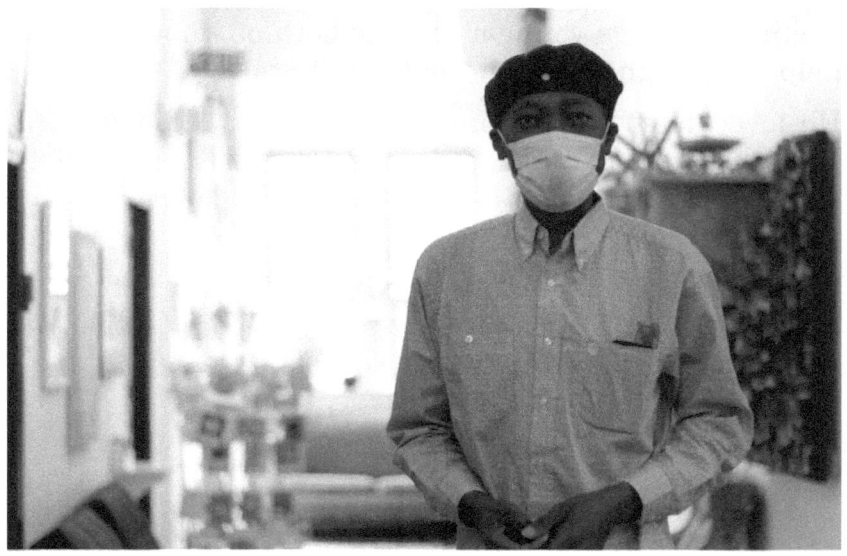

Semi Semi-Dikoko at Artwalk in 2021. Lucy Gellman File Photo.

Semi-Dikoko was born in Congo, the second oldest of four children to a nurse, Dorcas Wumba-Di-Mazimi, and Andre Kinsumba, an executive at the Central Bank of Congo. Before his birth, his mother studied at a nursing school run by American missionaries, then worked for the Ministry of Health and Ministry of Justice in Belgian Congo.

Because his father was out of the house so often, Semi-Dikoko became a kind of second father figure to his two younger sisters, who later moved with him to New Haven.

As a child, "Semi was special," his sister Annie Gumba said last Thursday afternoon, as family filled her home in Westville, and stories flitted through the kitchen and dining room. From a young age, he shouldered household responsibilities, busying himself in the kitchen, and then fixing things around the house. By the time he was in his early teens, he was doing the home's landscaping while looking after his younger sisters, both of whom he later helped through school in the United States.

He loved to cook, teaching himself to make beans, and later duck, cornish hen, fish, and Brussels sprouts with a pomegranate reduction that gained celebrity status across New Haven.

If something broke around the house, he would fix it. If he didn't know how to—in an age well before Google and video tutorials—he taught himself.

The mobiles that Sepulveda and Semi Semi-Dikoko built in their studio. Jadan Anderson File Photo.

It built the foundation for not just his professional work as a systems architect, but a life spent tinkering. As a teen, Semi-Dikoko played flute and trombone, sang, and had a love for opera and classical music that his cousins remembered as contagious (and indeed, the studio he shared with Sepulveda was often filled with music). Calling from Paris, his cousin Hyacinthe said that there was no subject too large or too daunting for Semi-Dikoko to navigate.

"He was *very* curious," Gumba said. "Learning *an-y-thing* that came around. At one point, we said, 'Are you an engineer? Are you a teacher? Are you a technician? He was up to everything! Seriously. Every single thing.'"

By the time he was in his 20s, he told his parents that he was going to take care of his two younger sisters—and he made good on his word. After securing a job as a computer analyst with IBM in Congo, he moved to Brussels, Belgium, and then to Bremen, Germany. When she was 16, Gumba joined him in Bremen. It was the beginning of a career that would take him from West Africa to Europe to the U.S.

In her older brother, she saw a gentleman who could jump from German to French to Japanese, slip into Bantu and Swahili, and steer conversations through politics, engineering, and the arts in a single night.

Semi Semi-Dikoko and his sister, Annie Gumba. David Sepulveda Photo.

Mostly, she saw how deeply he cared for the people and places around him. During their years in Bremen, the two would sometimes visit a restaurant that required punting a boat across a small lake. As he took the oars, she recalled, he often offered to do the work, and let her sit back in the boat.

That's just who he was, she said—always willing to make the ride a little easier for whoever was with him, and whoever might come next.

"A Catalyst for Creativity"

Sepulveda and Semi-Dikoko downtown. Thomas McMillan File Photo. The image below is a file photo from the New Haven Independent.

It was during those years that Semi-Dikoko's professional star was also rising. In the early 1980s, he worked on a joint project for the National Aeronautics and Space Administration (NASA) and the European International Space Agency (EISA) in Belgium that became a door to the U.S. After moving to New York City, he worked on Wall Street, then for a headhunting firm, then in software, recalled his friend and former colleague Steve Rubino.

There was nothing he couldn't do, said Rubino, who praised him for the creative thinking with which he often approached problems in the field. As the two traded stories about their work on Wall Street and in IT, they grew close. Decades of friendship later, Rubino often finds himself asking "what would Semi do?" In the last three years, the two were particularly close.

"He was a catalyst for creativity," he said in a phone call Tuesday night. "The goodness inside of him, you couldn't suppress it. He was always looking to better himself through art, and he loved what he did. I think he was a facilitator in a lot of ways ... He was one in a million."

It was consulting work with SNET that ultimately brought Semi-Dikoko to Connecticut, where he made New Haven his home in 1991. As he worked, he maintained that role as a sort of second father, helping Nkebani with her studies at St. Michael's College in Vermont as Gumba pursued a degree at Albertus Magnus College.

That was true even as he earned his pilot's license, and used his newfound aviation skills to serve those around him. Laughing at the memory, Gumba recalled how her brother would fly the two from New Haven to Long Island, in a successful attempt to bypass traffic on the highway as they headed to see their sister in Vermont. Years later when lymphoma grounded him, he would regale the impromptu, salon-like gatherings in his studio with stories of being in flight.

In New Haven he wore many hats (almost all of them red and black berets), from consultant to neighborhood booster to doting uncle, known and adored in his family's youngest circles simply as "Tonton Semi." When Gumba first got married, Semi-Dikoko helped her husband find work in the U.S., doing consulting in the Connecticut area. He became a dedicated uncle to Gumba's children, Christian Ngongi-Semi and Simone and Sarah Ngongi.

"Uncle Semi raised us," Sarah Ngongi said Thursday. "He really helped me explore my artistry. He definitely contributed to the woman that I am today, and my love for the arts."

After his move to the Elm City in the 1990s, Semi-Dikoko built an extended family of friends in New Haven, from the city's arts community to its nonprofit scene to local government. Goode, who met him in the early 2000s, remembered his friend as deeply insightful, with a clarity around the kind of advocacy work he wanted to do. Initially, the two were in a then-nascent Democracy School cohort together. They remained close until the end of Semi-Dikoko's life.

"I remember him telling me that he was interested in doing Democracy School because he wanted to learn the tools to become a better advocate for the arts," Goode said in a phone call Monday. "He had a great understanding of politics because he had a great understanding of life."

And he did. In 2010, Semi-Dikoko became president of the Friends of Edgewood Park, where he led New Haven in a nationwide contest to get fruit trees along the park's trails. The contest, titled "Communities Take Root," had over 120 entrants from some 20 towns and cities across the U.S. Semi-Dikoko wasn't phased: he enlisted the help of his friends, networks, and social media to get 33,000 New Haveners to sign. New Haven won by over 10,000 signatures.

"I felt like I was watching Churchill leading the British people during World War II," Goode said. It convinced him of the role that social media could play in spreading the word on civic projects and information, which he still does through his incisive, often funny Twitter presence.

Semi-Dikoko with the 2021 Thanksgiving meal he prepared for his family, while living in temporary housing. David Sepulveda Photo.

He was also a great calm in a greater storm, working to serve his community and family through tremendous heartbreak of his own. In 2011, his nephew Christian

Ngongi-Semi was killed by a drunk driver while walking on the shoulder of the road with a friend in East Haven. He was 16, with a sweet, boyish face and eyes that lit up a whole room. Semi-Dikoko, after whom Ngongi-Semi was affectionately named, was crushed.

"It was very hard for Semi," Gumba remembered. Shortly after his nephew's death, he was diagnosed with lymphoma for the first time.

Even in his own private pain, Semi-Dikoko didn't stop giving to New Haven. In the public eye, he helped plant those 48 fruit trees in Edgewood Park. At home, he supported his sister, finding the ways to care for his nieces as they grieved the loss of a brother, and for Gumba and her husband as they faced life without their son. He threw himself into planning committees, becoming involved with the then-young Westville Village Renaissance Alliance and early celebrations of the neighborhood's annual Westville Artwalk.

Sepulveda, whose daughter Kara was the same age as Ngongi-Semi, grew close with Semi-Dikoko during that time. When Semi-Dikoko was diagnosed with lymphoma in 2011, Sepulveda created a landscaping project that the two could do together at Gumba's home, nestled at the corner of Ray Road and Birch Drive in the city's Westville neighborhood.

There, Sepulveda remembered, the two would kneel in the grass, carry trays of flowers, and figure out tree-to-tree irrigation pathways that had them working for hours alongside each other. Semi-Dikoko, who loved nature, often joked that he was sweating the cancer out. Within years, the two became inseparable. On Tuesday, Sepulveda's wife, Priscilla Sepulveda, said that Semi-Dikoko was so loved in their home that even the dog, Georgia, will mourn his absence.

The Mayor Of Westville

Semi Semi-Dikoko with Artspace New Haven Former Director Helen Kauder at a Puerto Ricans United gala in 2018. Lucy Gellman File Photo.

In every direction a person looked—including his intimate, mobile-studded shared studio— Semi-Dikoko poured his energy into the community around him. In interviews for this piece, dozens of artists remembered him as the life of the party and the glue that often pulled them together. It did not matter where they met him—often at an exhibition opening, but sometimes simply on the street in Westville—they fell instantly in love with him.

Westvillian Aly Fox, whose "Friendsgiving " celebrations gained celebrity status in the neighborhood before the Covid-19 pandemic, remembered meeting Semi-Dikoko around 2012, when he rolled up to her apartment around eight or nine in the evening.

By then, most of her guests had moved on to dessert and coffee. Semi-Dikoko brought a tray of Brussels sprouts, still on the stalk, bathed in a pomegranate reduction and sprinkled with pomegranate seeds. He danced with guests, a glass of red wine almost always cradled in his hand as he moved. As he returned year after year, it became his signature.

"That was just one of the ongoing jokes of Friendsgiving, like it wasn't complete until Semi brought the Brussels sprouts," she said. "And it wasn't complete until there was dancing with Semi. The life of the party was him, and it wasn't a party until he was with you."

As they got to know each other, she said, she was struck by the lack of hierarchy in his life. If you shared "a meal and a glass of wine," you were part of that growing, extended family. When she found out he had passed, Fox said she wanted to tell the neighborhood to go into Edgewood Park with their wine and food, and raise a glass in his honor.

At home, *Tonton* Semi remained the same supportive presence he had always been. When he learned that fashion helped Sarah cope with her brother's death, he encouraged her to pursue it. From her classes at Cooperative Arts and Humanities High School to her fledgling fashion brand Avec Dieu, he became her loudest and most steadfast cheerleader.

Sam Dapper and Sarah Ngongi at Seeing Sounds earlier this year. Lucy Gellman File Photo.

As she grew up, he nurtured that spark, giving her a workspace in his shared studio. After years on the planning committee for Artwalk New Haven, he introduced her to some of its fellow artist-organizers, from Mistina and Luke Hanscom to Mohamad Hafez and Susan McCaslin, with whom he shared a floor at West River Arts.

In May, Sarah watched as he and Sepulveda took their seats in the first row of a fashion show where she was presenting her work.

"The majority of the time I would be happy, but if I knew there was a feeling that I can't shake, I would go to my sewing machine and try a design," she said. "Uncle Semi ... he would always tell me, 'I'm a consultant, come to me! If you need some guidance, I'm here.'"

By then, Semi-Dikoko had very much become the unofficial mayor of Westville—and sometimes, it seemed, of New Haven—many times over. If a visitor stumbled into his studio (as this reporter often did), it was Semi-Dikoko who offered them a glass of red wine or, if it was late at night and he needed to stay awake, a pot of black coffee. Because he worked with international clients, he was often awake into the wee hours of the morning.

It was, and will continue to be, a magical space. Inside, he and Sepulveda assembled mobiles from recycled laundry detergent containers, turning the thick plastic, colorful into Calder-esque designs that caught in the light and could transport a viewer instantly back to childhood. Early in the process, Semi-Dikoko figured out a way to balance the plastic shapes with alligator clips, fixed to the strings just so.

Semi Semi-Dikoko and Kim Weston in his studio. David Sepulveda Photo.

To ease Sepulveda's trigger wrist, Semi-Dikoko also began to research and then use the CNC process, using it to cut out plastic shapes at MakeHaven. That was Semi, Sepulveda said: fascinated by a complex process, and eager to learn it if it helped a friend.

"He would come back with a table full of beautiful shapes and then he started making cuts within a shape, opening within the mobile shape," Sepulveda said. "It just added so much to that mobile design."

Under his watchful eye, the studio became a gathering place, where conversation flowed freely and laughter rose in thick, weightless clouds through the air. Semi-Dikoko could talk about anything, peppering his sentences with *darling* and *mon ami* and toward the end of the night, a kiss on the cheek.

"It was like being at an 18th-century French salon," Goode said. "The wine would flow and the conversation would flow, and we'd just bask in his radiance, his effervescence, his connoisseurship of art and life."

It was not just his warmth that drew people to him, but his willingness to give counsel freely and without reservation. When Mistina and Luke Hanscom bought the buildings that [would become Lotta Studio and West River Arts](#) in 2015, Semi-Dikoko urged them "to think bigger" in their fundraising. Mistina, who for years worked alongside him coordinating Artwalk, grew to love their conversations.

"I'm not sure I remember life without Semi," she said. "I could just show up at his studio door and sit on his floor. He was very easily accessible, and I think that that was one of the most beautiful qualities. His door was always open, and he never shied away from difficult conversations. He just provided a different perspective."

"I never passed by his door and saw him in a bad mood," said the artist [Mohamad Hafez](#), a fellow night owl who works in studio next door, and often welcomed Semi-Dikoko's late night visits. During 2016 and 2017, Semi-Dikoko helped pull Hafez through the emotional anguish and stress of the early Trump years as he channeled them into his art. "He was just really, a lit up person. His energy was very contagious. It was very hard to be around him and be sad and miserable."

That was true across the city, where Semi-Dikoko endeared himself to every organization, friend, and later hospital employee he met. Roughly seven years ago, Semi-Dikoko joined the board of Artspace New Haven, on which he actively served until his death. Former Artspace Director Helen Kauder, who stepped back from the organization in 2020, stressed how strongly he worked to build bridges between Westville, downtown New Haven, and the rest of the city.

She estimated that she was on the phone with him "at least once a week," brainstorming about how to better fund and support not just Artspace, but all of the arts in New Haven.

"It Was Like My King Had Passed"

Susan Clinard and Semi Semi-Dikoko. David Sepulveda Photo. The image below, of Clinard's bust, is by Susan Clinard.

Even as Semi-Dikoko's body failed him, his mind remained clear. Six years ago, he moved in with Gumba, who formed a sort of dynamic care duo with Sepulveda. When a fire erupted in their Birch Drive home 18 months ago and displaced the family—all during his cancer treatments—he didn't let it dampen his spirits.

Last Thanksgiving, he prepared a meal while the family was living in transitional Yale graduate student housing downtown. When the family moved back in months ago, his whole presence filled the space.

Thursday, Gumba said she thinks of that time as giving back: she was able to do some of the cooking and caretaking that he had done for her and then her children decades before.

"He was really a father to me, and I had to give it back to him, that's why I kept him under my roof," she said in an interview at her home in Westville. "I'm really grateful that I spent the time with him. He fought. He wanted to live. He's a fighter. There was no winning with this [cancer]."

He spent his final months, and then weeks, delighting the community he so loved, and that he had made his home. In May, the artist Susan Clinard began laying the groundwork for a bust of Semi-Dikoko, which she completed in August. Sepulveda, who was rarely not by his friend's side, documented the process.

After meeting him six years ago, when she was curating *Stories from Far and Near* at the New Haven Museum, she called it one of the greatest honors of her career. During her work curating the show, Semi-Dikoko had stepped in to translate for writer and theatermaker Toto Kisaku, then an asylum seeker newly in the United States. The two became fast friends.

In the finished piece, his eyes travel up and to the left, as if he is watching a bird soar across the sky. One of his signature berets rests atop his head. It is crown-like for a reason: Semi-Dikoko was regal.

"For a sculptor, there's nothing more amazing, more sweet than having someone sit for a portrait," she said in a phone call last Thursday afternoon. "It was a beautiful time with Semi, where we sculpted this together. I say we sculpted *together* because his beautiful self just seeped into my fingertips.I feel so blessed that we had those intimate, joyful hours that we got to spend together in this studio."

Photographer and educator Kim Weston, the driving force behind Wábi Gallery, also spoke to him during that time. In a phone call Sunday, she estimated that she'd known Semi-Dikoko for 15 years, and worked closely with him for many of those ("his studio was the place to *be*," she said with a smile somewhere in her voice).

In May, she stepped back from board leadership at Artspace for professional reasons. He called her just to check in, and give the counsel for which he was so well known. It was the last time they spoke.

"He said, 'go build Wábi,'" she recalled. "You came to New Haven to build. You go build that, because New Haven needs you. Needs people like you. Needs *artists* like you. For New Haven Haven artists, and for artists all around."

When she found out he had died on Thursday, "it was like my king had passed," she said. "I felt like that was such a loss of a soul. A soul of a man."

There was not a person who met Semi-Dikoko and did not fall in love with him. When he received chemo on his 69th birthday, nurses serenaded him as Sepulveda recorded in the background. In a video from that day, Semi-Dikoko is holding a cupcake the size of his palm, the plastic lid fitted over a crown of white and green frosting.

Five nurses surround his chair, their hands clapping as they sing. His eyes follow them, and even beneath a mask it is clear that he is summoning a smile. At the end of the song, he lifts the box to his mouth in gratitude, then blows a kiss with his left hand.

In the days since his death, both Gumba and Sepulveda have listened as story after story emerges, all of them told with the same warmth with which Semi-Dikoko lived his life. Some friends sent poems about Brussels sprouts and dancing. Others recalled his famous toasts, from Artspace to Artwalk to the studio where he held court.

In his absence, both Weston and Mistina Hanscom said that his legacy will be passing that generous spirit on to others, particularly to young artists.

At the end, he was not alone. When he moved into the ICU last week, family stayed with him for hours on end. In his final moments, Ziner reminded him how loved he was. She is just one of dozens, if not hundreds, now grappling with what many called simply a "Semi-sized hole" that has been ripped in their chests.

"He took up a room," Weston said. "He was the center of attention, but he would turn it back around to whatever artist needed it. That's what made him the mayor of New Haven. And he's going to be missed in so many areas. He was a profound soul, and he was good at everything that he did. He found the good in everybody."

From Vietnam – The Lucky Few --- the Rest of the Story

... Hugh Doyle, former chief engineer aboard the USS Kirk FF1087, lives near Newport Rhode Island; as a retired Navy veteran, he receives his medical care from the Naval Health Clinic at the Newport Naval Station. When he recently went to the clinic for a checkup, he learned that his regular Navy physician had been reassigned and that a new physician, Lt. Cdr. Khan Van Nguyen, would he his primary care doctor. At his first appointment Doyle asked his new physician when, and how he and his family left Vietnam; he surmised that they may have been "boat people" a second wave of refugees who fled Vietnam in the late 1970s and early 1980s.

Nguyen responded that he really didn't know about the family's exodus since he was a baby at the time. Moreover, his father had since died without ever relating the story to him. Doyle gave the doctor a copy of The Lucky Few DVD, which Nguyen watched with his wife. Although Nguyen related to Doyle that he was moved by the film, he was none the wiser about his own history.

Dr. Nguyen's large family had settled in the San Francisco bay area and flourished. Khan, the youngest of five children, recalled that his family never discussed their flight from Vietnam. After he watched the documentary, Khan talked intermittently with his mother and siblings, asking them more probing questions. The only information he could gather at the time was that they left Saigon on a large Vietnamese navy ship. His sister insisted that she remembered it had a large "1" painted on the hull. She also recalled that the ship went to an island and joined up with other ships heading for the Philippines.

Dr. Nguyen's sister and brother-in-law visited with him during a trip east to enroll their daughter at Boston College. During that stopover Khan showed them "The Lucky Few" film and described their awed reaction: "They were blown away!" Since that time, Dr. Nguyen has been able to determine that his family escaped on HQ-1, which was part of a larger formation. His sister, who was a young teenager at the time, clearly remembered the re-flagging ceremony and Kirk's motor whaleboat coming alongside HQ-1 to deliver food, water and medicine. Dr. Nguyen told Doyle that the film was an incredibly emotional experience for his sister and that the memories came flooding back to her.

Shortly after learning how the film had psychologically impacted Dr. Nguyen's family, Doyle hosted a public showing of The Lucky Few at his church's parish center. He introduced Dr. Nguyen, who, he had since learned, was not only a member of the same church but was a one-year-old boy on one of the ships (Tran Hung Dao [HQ-1]) in the documentary!

"What are the odds" Doyle asked in utter astonishment, "that that one-year-old boy would survive the war, escape from Vietnam with his family, come to the United States, attend medical school, join the Navy, be stationed at the Newport Naval Station, and become my doctor?"

The Rest of the Story – To Distant Shores

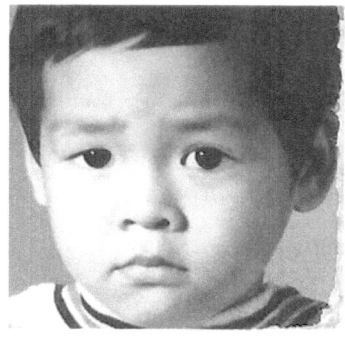 

The story of USS Kirk and The Lucky Few always leaves me with feelings of pride in those young sailors on that small Navy ship. And seeing and hearing the gratitude of those rescued often brings a tear to my mostly dry eyes.

But the story of that rescue is just a part of the story of those rescued. What are the lifelong stories that surround that relatively short episode at sea?

What are the stories of those many thousands whose stories encompass war, struggles for life, life in a new county and a new culture so different from the land they lost and left behind?

To Distant Shores[2] *is one* such story published recently. The story is a blend of remembrances of an 8-year-old boy

---

[22] To Distant Shores: Phan, Huan, Phan, Tiep: https://www.amazon.com/Distant-Shores-Huan-

and those of his father, a South Vietnamese Naval officer. The blended story tells an end-to-end story of: life in Vietnam; war; fear; escape; survival; transport across a vast sea; and finally assimilation of a family into the fabric of America. Note that the 8-year-old author is now a Ph.D. Bio- chemist researcher.

Phan/dp/B0BBXQQY9Q/ref=tmm_pap_swatch_0?_encoding=UTF8&qid=1696697645&sr=1-4

Here is an excerpt from the book. In context, at their final destination in San Diego County, a church congregation provided the family with a fully furnished home. The following is a testimony given by author Tiếp Phan.

Two days later, as previously planned, we attended services at the church where we would be introduced to the parishioners. I asked for a chance to express my gratitude. In front of the altar, I said, "Dear Father, ladies, and gentlemen. It is an honor and a great surprise for me today to have the chance to stand here, in the light of God, to express my gratitude to you all." The hall was already loudly clapping. I continued,

Phan, Huan ; Phan, Tiep. To Distant Shores (p. 147). Phan Lac Press. Kindle Edition.

... When we left Vietnam, communists were about to enter Sài Gòn. More than 5,000 people piled onto a broken ship. None of us believed that it could leave the harbor. But it did leave port, and that was a miracle. We traveled down the narrow Sài Gòn River, both sides of which were battlegrounds, but we made it out safely. That was another miracle. When Sài Gòn fell into enemy hands, we were still stuck at the river mouth, but eventually, we managed to escape to the open sea. That was a miracle ... And finally, we were saved by an American navy ship [USS Kirk], putting an end to the horrors of that broken and crowded vessel. That was again a miracle. I believe that it was God saving us. God has guided us from danger to a safe haven so that our family could be here today, before His light and in the embracing arms of Father and all of you. That is again a miracle. Thanks be to God, and thank you ..."

This episode adds to my pride in America and the kinds of people we are capable of being.

Another Viet Nam Immigrant

On Saturday, July 24th, 2010 the town of Prescott Valley, AZ, hosted a Freedom Rally. Quang Nguyen was asked to speak on his experience of coming to America and what it means. He spoke the following in dedication to all Viet Nam Veterans. Thought you might enjoy hearing what he had to say:

Quang Nguyen first came to America as a war refugee with a small bag of clothes on his back. Thanks to what makes America the greatest country on earth, he is now a successful small-business owner and prominent public speaker, with a son working in the private sector and a daughter in her third year as a Midshipman at the U.S. Naval Academy in Annapolis, Maryland.

"35 years ago, if you were to tell me that I am going to stand up here speaking to a couple thousand patriots, in English, I'd laugh at you. Man, every morning I wake up thanking God for putting me and my family in the greatest country on earth.

"I just want you all to know that the American dream does exist and I am living the American dream. I was asked to speak to you about my experience as a first generation Vietnamese- American, but I'd rather speak to you as an American.

"If you hadn't noticed, I am not white and I feel pretty comfortable with my people.

"I am a proud US citizen and here is my proof. It took me 8 years to get it, waiting in endless lines, but I got it, and I am very proud of it.

"I still remember the images of the Tet offensive in 1968, I was six years old. Now you might want to question how a 6-year-old boy could remember anything. Trust me, those images can never be erased. I can't even imagine what it was like for young American soldiers, 10,000 miles away from home, fighting on my behalf.

"35 years ago, I left South Viet Nam for political asylum. The war had ended. At the age of 13, I left with the understanding that I may or may not ever get to see my siblings or parents again. I was one of the first lucky 100,000 Vietnamese allowed to come to the US . Somehow, my family and I were reunited 5 months later, amazingly, in California. It was a miracle from God.

"If you haven't heard lately that this is the greatest country on earth, I am telling you that right now. It was the freedom and the opportunities presented to me that put me here with all of you tonight. I also remember the barriers that I had to overcome every step of the way. My high school counselor told me that I cannot make it to college due to my poor communication skills. I proved him wrong. I finished college. You see, all you have to do is to give this little boy an opportunity and encourage him to take and run with it. Well, I took the opportunity and here I am.

"This person standing tonight in front of you could not exist under a socialist/ communist environment. By the way, if you think socialism is the way to go, I am sure many people here will chip in to get you a one-way ticket out of here. And if you didn't know, the only difference between socialism and communism is an AK-47 aimed at your head. That was my experience.

"In 1982, I stood with a thousand new immigrants, reciting the Pledge of Allegiance and listening to the National Anthem for the first time as an American. To this day, I can't remember anything sweeter and more patriotic than that moment in my life.

"Fast forwarding, somehow, I finished high school, finished college, and like any other goofball 21 year old kid, I was having a great time with my life. I had a nice job and a nice apartment in Southern California. In some way and somehow, I had forgotten how I got here and why I was here.

"One day I was at a gas station, I saw a veteran pumping gas on the other side of the island. I don't know what made me do it, but I walked over and asked if he had served in Viet Nam . He smiled and said yes. I shook and held his hand. The grown man began to well up. I walked away as fast as I could and at that very moment, I was emotionally rocked. This was a profound moment in my life. I knew something had to change in my life. It was time for me to learn how to be a good citizen. It was time for me to give back.

"You see, America is not just a place on the map, it isn't just a physical location. It is an ideal, a concept. And if you are an American, you must understand the concept, you must accept this concept, and most importantly, you have to fight and defend this concept. This is about Freedom and not free stuff. And that is why I am standing up here.

"Brothers and sisters, to be a real American, the very least you must do is to learn English and understand it well. In my humble opinion, you cannot be a faithful patriotic citizen if you can't speak the language of the country you live in. Take this document of 46 pages – last I looked on the Internet, there wasn't a Vietnamese translation of the US Constitution. It took me a long time to get to the point of being able to converse and until this day, I still struggle to come up with the right words. It's not easy, but if it's too easy, it's not worth doing.

"Before I knew this 46-page document, I learned of the 500,000 Americans who fought for this little boy. I learned of the 58,000 names scribed on the black wall at the Viet Nam Memorial. You are my heroes. You are my founders.

"At this time, I would like to ask all the Viet Nam veterans to please stand. I thank you for my life. I thank you for your sacrifices, and I thank you for giving me the freedom and liberty I have today. I now ask all veterans, firefighters, and police officers, to please stand. On behalf of all first generation immigrants, I thank you for your services and may God bless you all."

Quang Nguyen

Creative Director/Founder

Caddis Advertising, LLC

Notice that he referred to himself as an American, NOT Vietnamese – American.

How good it would be here in America if all of the immigrants—no, EVERYONE — felt like Quang Nguyen.

"God Bless America "

"One Flag, One Language, One Nation Under God"

From Romania

Source: Romanian immigrant to Americans who favor communism: 'If you don't learn from history, nothing will save you'

https://www.foxnews.com/politics/romanian-immigrant-to-americans-who-favor-communism

Romanian immigrant to Americans who favor communism: 'If you don't learn from history, nothing will save you'

Immigrant from former Soviet-occupied nation shocked to find communism growing in America

A Romanian immigrant who moved to the United States in pursuit of a better life said Americans favoring communism need to learn from history or "nothing will save you."

"I'm not saying that every system in the world is perfect, but to be in favor of communism, considering history and everything that has been documented throughout the years, it's sad. It's really sad," Bogdan Laurentiu told Fox News.

Laurentiu, 34, moved from Romania, which was previously occupied by the Soviet Union, to the U.S. with a friend in 2010, leaving his entire family behind. He works in retail management, lives in the Northeast and says he has "no regrets to this day."

He said he made more sacrifices than he could count in order to succeed in the U.S. But after a decade in the U.S. he said he feels, "very grateful, very honored to be here and to have the opportunity to live in America."

A Soviet-sponsored youth rally in the Lustgarten in Berlin, Germany, 1st June 1950. The youth carry huge portraits of Communist leaders such as Joseph Stalin (pictured). (FPG/Getty Images)

"People all across the globe see America as a beacon of freedom and a beacon of hope," Laurentiu told Fox News. But he added that loud criticism from American media and the political left have affected the superpower's reputation.

Laurentiu said the most shocking surprise he encountered since moving to the U.S. was learning that a growing number of Americans favor communism.

"If anybody would have told me before I came to America there would come a day when I would encounter or meet American citizens in favor of communism, I probably would have laughed in their face," he said.

West Berlin citizens continue their vigil atop the Berlin Wall in front of the Brandeburg Gate in this November 10, 1989 file photo. The 10th anniversary off the "fall" of the Berlin wall is coming up on November 9, 1999. (REUTERS)

Laurentiu said the memory of living under Soviet rule is still fresh in the minds of eastern Europeans.

"In my 24 years of living in Romania, I have not heard one person talk positively about communism," he said.

"But when you talk with people here about it and you tell them about ... the lived experiences of people that lived under communism and how life was there ... they tell you that you don't know what you're talking about," Laurentiu told Fox News.

"We're not talking about socialism here. We are talking about actual leftists that are in favor of communism and everything that that entails ... because they read a theory," he said, referring to Karl Marx's Communist Manifesto.

In this Oct. 24, 1956 file photo, people gather around a fallen statue of Soviet leader Josef Stalin in front of the National Theater in Budapest, Hungary.

The uprising in Hungary began on Oct. 23, 1956 with demonstrations against the Stalinist regime in Budapest and was crushed eleven days later by Soviet tanks amid bitter fighting. For Hungary, a pro-Russian leader in the White House offers hope the Western world might end the sanctions imposed over Russia's annexation of Crimea and its role in eastern Ukraine. Many Poles, instead, fear a U.S-Russian rapprochement under Trump could threaten their own security interests. To most Poles, NATO represents the best guarantee for an enduring independent state in a difficult geographical neighborhood. (Arpad Hazafi/Associated Press)

Laurentiu was never interested in politics until the defund the police movement became popular across the nation in 2020. It prompted him to look more closely at political forces within the country.

He now runs a political commentary TikTok account, "The Conservative Immigrant," which has over 110,000 followers.

"It's very important for us to learn history," Laurentiu said. "And not just a part of history that suits our narrative."

"A lot of people are just woke because it's trendy, because it's popular ... rather than having a little bit of critical thinking and acknowledging everything that this country is offering," he told Fox News. "The system is not perfect. I'll be the first one to admit that. It's not perfect. But if you put your mind to it, the impossible can happen."

From Turkey

Source: AP Photo/Mary Schwalm

Source: https://townhall.com/tipsheet/leahbarkoukis/2021/12/10/enes-kanter-freedom-oped-n2600421

Full of Pride for America, Enes Kanter Freedom Explains Why He Became a US Citizen

Enes Kanter Freedom (he changed his last name upon recently receiving U.S. citizenship) is a breath of fresh air amid the seemingly constant public scorn for America we hear from activists, celebrities, and progressive politicians.

In a piece for The Atlantic, the Boston Celtics player who gained prominence recently for speaking out against human rights abuses explains why he loves America so much and decided to become a citizen.

Growing up in Turkey, where President Recep Tayyip Erdogan has been ruling as an authoritarian since 2014, Freedom experienced firsthand the government's wrath against those who dared to speak out.

When I first arrived in the United States, I had to adjust to a new language, new norms, and new traditions. But I was perhaps most stunned by a simple comment a teammate made. He criticized President Barack Obama, which I feared could have landed him in prison. He smiled and said: "This isn't Turkey, brother. You have the freedom to say whatever you want."

Americans might find the thought absurd, but the threat of prison is all too real for those living under authoritarian rule around the world. (*The Atlantic*)

He explained how his parents publicly disowned him, that his dad eventually was jailed, and his siblings were blocked from employment.

And he, too, could've wound up getting jailed or worse.

"In 2017, on a basketball trip to Indonesia, I received a tip to leave the country immediately, to avoid a suspected kidnapping attempt by Turkish agents," he wrote. "On the next leg of our trip, in Europe, I was informed by border control that Turkey had revoked my citizenship. I would later learn that the regime had also issued an international arrest warrant against me.

"I was stranded. I had no family. I had no nationality. I had no home," he added.

But that's when America opened the door, and since then, he's taken full advantage of the First Amendment.

"When I started the process of becoming an American citizen, I realized that life is bigger than basketball. I decided to dedicate the power and privilege of my platform to the causes that matter—to be a voice for the voiceless," he said. "Yet far too many celebrities, athletes, and corporations still choose their money over their morals."

He ended the piece by writing about how much pride he has in his new citizenship.

"For six long years, I was without a home. I know what it's like for a people to have their freedom stripped away. And I know what it's like to have my own freedom stripped away. But this week, I'm reclaiming my Freedom. I just became an American citizen, and I'm making America and its freedoms a part of my very identity," he said.

"I'm overwhelmed with emotion just writing these words: I, Enes Kanter Freedom, am proud to be a citizen of the United States of America, the land of the free, and home of the brave."

From North Korea

Pictured above is Mr. Ji Seong-ho, an escapee from the brutality of North Korea. Read his account as told by

President Donald Trump in his 2018 State of the Union Address.³

Though not a refugee immigrant to the United States, the story of Mr. Ji Seong-ho resonates with those stories I have captured in this short book. There are many more, and as time marches on more such stories will be discovered.

Listen with your mind, your heart, and your soul as you hear this story.

"In 1996, Seong-ho was a starving boy in North Korea. One day, he tried to steal coal from a railroad car to barter for a few scraps of food. In the process, he passed out on the train tracks, exhausted from hunger. He woke up as a train ran over his limbs. He then endured multiple amputations without anything to dull the pain. His brother and sister gave what little food they had to help him recover and ate dirt themselves -- permanently stunting their own growth. Later, he was tortured by North Korean authorities after returning from a brief visit to China. His tormentors wanted to know if he had met any Christians. He had -- and he resolved to be free.

Seong-ho traveled thousands of miles on crutches across China and Southeast Asia to freedom. Most of his family followed. His father was caught trying to escape and was tortured to death.

Today he lives in Seoul, where he rescues other defectors, and broadcasts into North Korea what the regime fears the most – the truth.

---

[3] **Ji Seong ho** (born 1982) is a North Korean defector who lives in South Korea, where he works to raise awareness about the situation in North Korea and to help fellow defectors. He was badly injured by a train but managed to escape North Korea.
Read more at: https://en.wikipedia.org/wiki/Ji_Seong-ho

Today he has a new leg, but Seong-ho, I understand you still keep those crutches as a reminder of how far you have come. Your great sacrifice is an inspiration to us all.

Seong-ho's story is a testament to the yearning of every human soul to live in freedom.

From Yugoslavia *(where's that?)*

Source: As Arizona's attorney general and a first generation American, I'm grateful for the USA

https://www.foxnews.com/opinion/arizona-attorney-general-first-generation-american-grateful-usa?cmpid=fb_fnc&fbclid=IwAR0o2T7UcDNCwf0Jql_-ig8wMKIzIZHPHgR5ovuNGpsDiqRftTzF4KwDiGE

As Arizona's attorney general and a first generation American, I'm grateful for the USA.

This Thanksgiving, we can resolve to be the spark that strengthens our society.

Outrage and ingratitude are the currencies of today's society. Many people rush to take offense at the tiniest issue or express their discontent with any perceived slight. Unfortunately, our children and grandchildren are learning from our attitudes and will take our negativity to greater heights. This spiral is destructive to every unit of our society and will ultimately lead to the undoing of this country.

It is incumbent upon all of us to stop this cycle of outrage and ingratitude – especially as it pertains to the United States. This Thanksgiving, we can resolve to be the spark that strengthens our society. Instead of continuously looking for a reason to be outraged, we can choose to be grateful for what this country has given us and our families.

I have a unique perspective for being thankful for this country. My family fled communism from the former Yugoslavia. They came to America because this nation could provide them and their descendants with boundless opportunities and freedoms. They understood that the rule of law was the way of life here and that their rights would be protected.

There are many other countries around the world with constitutions or other founding documents that appear to grant protections or freedoms for their citizens. Without adherence to the rule of law, however, those documents mean absolutely nothing – as we've seen throughout world history. My family understood that the United States was different in this respect, and I'm thankful for what this nation stands for and the efforts its leaders undertake to enforce the rule of law.

My experience, combined with my family's history, has strengthened my gratitude for our nation and my resolve to give back and to serve our communities.

Nevertheless, the United States isn't perfect, and its opportunities for improvement are often magnified by people who have nothing but contempt for this country. Yet, the reality is that no other nation in history has been able to match what we have accomplished and the freedoms we've maintained and protected for hundreds of years. The United States has brought more opportunities to more people than any other country. My life is Exhibit A of this fact.

I often think about my hypothetical life if my parents hadn't fled communism to come to America. I would have little – if any – of the opportunities I have been given. My daughters would not have the freedoms they currently enjoy. My family is not alone with this "what-if" scenario. Millions of families have a similar story of their sacrifices and determination in pursuing the American Dream.

Then I consider my life as it stands now, and I can be nothing but thankful. My family had the courage to immigrate to this country. I was given an opportunity to be educated and obtain my law degree. I was honored to serve as a JAG officer in the U.S. Army. I met my wife when we both worked as prosecutors, and we have been blessed with two daughters. I have been honored to serve as a federal and state prosecutor, helping to protect our communities and enforce the rule of law that is the backbone of our society. I was fortunate to be elected Arizona's chief law enforcement officer.

Only here could this be the reality of a first-generation American whose first language is not even English. My experience, combined with my family's history, has strengthened my gratitude for our nation and my resolve to give back and to serve our communities. While we work to create a more perfect union, we must never forget that America remains the most extraordinary place to pursue a better life for more people than we could ever imagine.

This Thanksgiving, let us resolve to be truly grateful for everything we have been given. No matter who we are, what we look like, or where we came from, we are all Americans. We are united in our humanity and our appreciation that our rights are not given to us by other people but given to us by our Creator. And that we have an obligation to fight for all that is good and pass on to our children and grandchildren a nation they can continue to believe in and be thankful for.

Afghan doctor's family endures Taliban beatings

"I want to contribute something to this country"

Credit: https://www.foxnews.com/world/afghan-doctors-family-endures-taliban-beatings?cmpid=fb_fnc&fbclid=IwAR03ivcVvMlCt8YIUN_tURshz4dqxBFzOplzQQCQBDrluIuzGizDURuk-VYDr.

Dr. Wais Aria is a medical doctor and human rights activist whose work focused on treating trauma in children and women, including child soldiers.

Wais Aria, his wife and their four children were evacuated and have returned to their home in Virginia

Dr. Wais Aria, an Afghan human rights activist whose work centers on treating women and children who have survived trauma from terrorism, war and domestic violence, barely made it out of Kabul with his own family after Taliban fighters assaulted him multiple times outside the airport.

But now, separated from TABISH, the nonprofit he founded with just a donated laptop and built into an NGO with its own office building and 350 employees, he's already trying to give back in the U.S.

"People treat me as a refugee…burdening the shoulder of government," the soft-spoken but animated medical doctor told Fox News Friday. "But as a human being, I want to contribute something with this country, with this nation – that is the first goal for me."

Aria and his wife are Afghan nationals with green cards who have lived in Virginia since 2017. The youngest of their four children is an American citizen, and they went back to Afghanistan earlier this summer to visit relatives and so Aria could do work for his NGO.

"We never thought that the country, the regime would collapse," he said.

And [President Biden's](#) abrupt withdrawal of U.S. troops left them shocked when the news reached them at a relative's home.

"One of our colleagues told us how the situation was very tense, 'There's news that Kabul collapsed and the Taliban captured it,'" Aria said. "I said, 'What do you mean?'"

A happy stay with extended family turned into "concern and disaster," he said, as he, his wife and their children went into hiding. They feared for their safety because of their ties to the U.S. and his work with TABISH, which has partnered with USAID and other Western organizations.

And other relatives who worked with his nonprofit remain in Afghanistan and in hiding, he said, and some have blamed his work for causing them danger.

"I told them I did not do anything wrong – I helped people," he said. "Thousands of people, I brought positive change on the lives of children and women."

He also paid salaries to hundreds of workers, who in turn supported their own families, and the Taliban takeover uprooted all of that, with reports of militants going door to door and disappearing people with ties to the U.S.

After several days of moving from place to place, the State Department sent him an email telling him which airport gate to go to and when, Aria said.

But his documents meant nothing to Taliban militants manning checkpoints outside Kabul's airport, he said. Some of them couldn't even read and couldn't tell the difference between regular ID cards and passports.

On multiple occasions, when he asked to pass, he was beaten and forced back, he said. On one attempt, his daughter fainted. At another point, they made it to the gate but were denied entry and spent days waiting in the street.

After one beating, Aria said he was ready to give up on leaving and try to find a place to hide. But his brother talked him out of it.

"He said, 'If you stay here, it would be a risk for you, for your children, for me and for our family,'" Aria said. "So...in any scenario, you have to get out of this country, you don't have any other choice."

He finally made it through the gate, took the 45-minute walk to the terminal, caught a flight to Qatar, then to Germany, and ultimately back to the U.S.

But now safe in Virginia, he said he's uncertain about what to do next. As someone whose entire life has been dedicated to helping those less fortunate, he said he doesn't want to be viewed as a refugee.

"I have a lot of skills I can contribute for the betterment of this country," he said.

So he's already partnering with a new group in the U.S. to provide mental health support, English classes and other programs to evacuees.

There are tens of thousands of special immigrant visa recipients who fled Taliban rule in the past few weeks. Aria said his "big ambition" is to help guide them into fitting in, finding work and living normal lives.

"More support in order that they be able to work in this country and live their normal life," he said, "not to depend just on country benefits or just to ask [for] donations."

He said it's a complicated effort and he's not sure yet how he'll accomplish his goals – but it's his new American dream.

Afghanistan - again

A Los Angeles woman invited an Afghan refugee family over for Thanksgiving. Here's what happened at their first Thanksgiving meal

By [Natasha Chen](#), CNN

Updated 12:11 PM ET, Mon November 29, 2021

Asghary's family enjoys its first Thanksgiving meal.

(CNN) For his family's first experience with a traditional Thanksgiving meal, Wahidullah Asghary had to explain to his children what turkey is: "I said, 'turkey is like a big chicken.'"

Asghary, a former translator and interpreter for the US military in [Afghanistan](#), came to the United States on a special immigrant visa in September 2020. He brought his four children, who tried to learn English while enrolled in what was then all-virtual school at the time. His wife joined them five months later.

Thursday was the first time they had been invited by an American household to experience a Thanksgiving meal.

"Every homeland, every nation, every people, every person, they have got a culture or tradition, right? So it is our first time, and now we want to learn a little bit about what this is, really," Asghary said.

This pilot fled Afghanistan as a child. Now he's bringing Afghan refugees hope on their journey to America

Their host, Kiki Nagy, volunteers for Miry's List, a Southern California-based group that helps refugee families settle in the U.S. In August, during the U.S. withdrawal from Afghanistan, Miry's List enrolled more than 20 refugee families, about five times the number of families compared to the month before. Next year, the organization is working to prepare to help more than 300 families settle in Southern California.

Nagy had asked the organization's founder, Miry Whitehill, if she could host an Afghan family for their first Thanksgiving. She was connected with the Asgharys, whom she had never met until the day of the feast.

Nagy made a big turkey, cranberry sauce, potatoes and spinach. But she also prepared a halal lamb to make sure the Asghary family could have something familiar to eat. Asghary said his daughter, especially, liked all the food.

Nagy was eager to not only introduce them to Thanksgiving dishes, but to also show them the tradition of giving thanks.

"From the right and the left, everyone is kind of like, 'America has got problems -- x, y, z," Nagy said. "In the midst of this conflicting cultural moment, this narrative of division that we hear so much about, that there is something essential to the American experience that is rooted in gratitude, that is rooted in the volunteerism that you leave your country, you leave a situation and you come here with sometimes very little -- sometimes with nothing. And you start over. And you create this opportunity for your family."

Wahidullah Asghary.

Asghary said they have much to be thankful for: "We may have more opportunities in our life in our hands. So of course the foremost example is this, that we are together. Family."

He said they're lucky his wife was able to join them before so many others tried to make a chaotic exit in August during the U.S. withdrawal from Afghanistan.

The image of the many families trying to escape Afghanistan in August especially resonated with another guest at the same Thanksgiving party, Tam Van Tran.

Tran, a friend of Nagy's, was a refugee from Vietnam in 1975. Tran told CNN he and his siblings arrived in the U.S. one week before the fall of Saigon.

"When I saw the photo of the Afghans and the cargo plane, it reminded me very much of just -- I was in the same, but it was a gigantic cargo ship," Tran said.

When Tran came to California, he was about the same age as Asghary's oldest children. He said he and his siblings escaped initially without their parents, so they were welcomed in the home of Richard and Rejean Schulte, a foster family in Mountain View, California.

He said he could offer the Asgharys a warm welcome: "Brotherhood and camaraderie. In a sense, you know...I went through that experience in '75."

Like at many holiday gatherings across the country, several people at the table were at one point new to the country and had to learn American traditions. And many of them worked to seize the opportunity available in their new home country.

Asghary said he tells his children, "We are here for you, the United States is here for you, and everything you have got in your hand. What are you going to do is you have to study. That's it."

Nagy hopes one of their first lessons would be from their first Thanksgiving: "To see that that kind of tolerance is really possible in the United States and, um, I guess I would want them to feel, I would appreciate, that Americans are at heart, really a generous people."

From Ukraine as a child.

Karina Lipsman, is a Republican candidate for the US House of Representatives in Virginia.

Author's note: The following information is from her campaign literature. Although she is not yet a member of Congress, her story of immigration from Ukraine as a child is an inspirational story. Ukraine, a nation in the Former Soviet Union, has suffered much in her history, especially during WW-II under the brutality of Nazi Germany, and the Soviet Union. Such brutality and suffering continued following the war under the tyranny of the Communist Soviet Union. In recent days, Ukraine is fighting to retain her soverenty and liberty as yet another war rages with Russia.

That a poor child immigrant not yet speaking the language of her new nation has achieved such success, speaks volumes about her new nation – America.

A Product of the American Dream

I arrived in this country as a refugee from Ukraine when it was still part of the Soviet Union with my single mother and grandparents. We didn't speak English, survived on food stamps and lived in low income housing in Baltimore City. I remember my first day at public school, seeing my fellow students recite the Pledge of Allegiance, and not knowing a single word they were saying.

My mother played the role of both parents, while working as a seamstress to make ends meet and attending community college in the evenings to learn English and earn her bookkeeping certificate. Life was not easy but I learned from an early age the meaning of perseverance and hard work. I knew that because of my mother's sacrifices, I had the opportunity to make something of myself. I started working at the age of 14 at a local bagel shop and I've worked ever since.

American, by choice

As soon as I turned 18, I applied to be an American citizen. At my citizenship ceremony, I recited the most meaningful Pledge of Allegiance of my life and I knew in that moment just how fortunate I was to be given this opportunity that most people around the world can only dream of.

Academically and professionally accomplished

I completed my studies in 3 years with a Bachelor's degree in Economics while working full-time in the financial industry. After graduation, I joined the world of national defense and earned a Master's degree in engineering from The Johns Hopkins University while working full-time. After spending over a decade in the defense and intelligence communities, I voluntarily resigned to run for Congress.

Why I'm Running

Politicians in our current environment are out of touch and all you see is infighting instead of collaboration. It is my generation's time to get involved and change that toxic climate. As an immigrant from an oppressive regime, I don't take the freedoms in this nation for granted. It's my civic duty to get involved and support our society. That's why I'm running for Congress. To set an example of serving my nation, to represent my neighbors, and to leave the system better off for the next generation.

I have lived in Arlington, VA for almost a decade and I am living and experiencing the issues that we are all facing together in our community. As your Congresswoman, I will engage with everyone, regardless of party affiliation to represent your interests. I will prioritize introducing common sense solutions and work across the aisle for our district over engaging in partisan politics. I will advocate for common-sense policies that fight crime, reduce inflation, ease transportation and improve our educational standards.

Boat People

Eva Wojcik shared a photo
15h

If you're not old enough to remember the Boat People of Vietnam then this is definitely for your eyes.

September 4, 2015 Ho Chi Minh City, Vietnam

It's 1984 and my mother arrives in the UK with 89 other Vietnamese refugees known as the "boat people". With just the cloths on her back and her four children, she's confronted with the local people of a council estate. Unable to speak English, she expects hostility and racism.

And then this happens.

A young scruffy looking man steps up, takes off his coat and handed it to the freezing cold refugees. A gesture so touching, that everybody later followed.

People then went home to fetch clothes they didn't need and handed it to the refugees and ensured they were all fed and watered.

My mother has never forgot that moment, when she was able to use a coat to wrap her boys so they could stop shivering. My brother can still remember the warmth that coat gave him and it stays in his heart to this day.

It's these things that British people do, that make make them truly British.

My family has never forgotten what England has done for them.

And because you allowed us in, we were able to give so much back to your country.

You gave us free healthcare. My family gave you 3 doctors. One has recently started working at Southmead hospital.

We never stole your jobs, we created our own and gave some to you.

In my family, there are 10 nails shops, 3 restaurants and 14 Chinese takeaways. We did this to give you amazing food and so we could support ourselves.

Please take a moment to think about all the Syrian refugees and think to yourself,

what makes you British?

Stockton farmworker turned astronaut inspires

NASA astronaut José Hernández. (Image credit: NASA)

This is an interesting and inspiring story of a young farm worker who went on to great heights. José is a first-generation American whose family of migrant farm workers immigrated from Mexico. Though not a refugee as many of the others I have highlighted, the story of José is a vivid example of what can be accomplished within the twin pillars of Liberty and Opportunity provided by an exceptional nation.

Reference – search for:

"Stockton farmworker turned astronaut"

(FOX40.COM) — Outer space may reach *a million miles away* and beyond, but the story of José M oreno Hernández, a Stockton farmworker who went on to become an astronaut with NASA and made the trip into outer space will be on screens here on Earth at the start of Hispanic Heritage Month.

"I've coined the phase that it's going to become an instant inspirational classic," Hernández told FOX40.com in a recent interview. "I'm hoping that my words come to fruition."

Hernández said he is a first-generation American whose family immigrated from Mexico. He spent his childhood working in the fields in San Joaquin County alongside his family, but he always dreamed of reaching the stars. A movie inspired by Hernández's life and journey to space called "A Million Miles Away" can be seen on Amazon Prime.

"When I was 10 years old I saw the very last Apollo mission – Apollo 17, and I was mesmerized," Hernández said. "I saw astronaut Gene Cernan walking on the moon. Every 10-year-old during that era wanted to be an astronaut and I too wanted to be an astronaut."

Little did he know – that childhood dream would one day become a reality, but not without some struggle. Hernández said the desire to be an astronaut stuck with him throughout his life, leading to his application to be a part of NASA's program, but he was rejected 11 times.

Hernandez said there were times that he felt like giving up, especially after being turned down so many times.

"I had doubts. No one likes rejection. Being rejected 11 times takes its toll," Hernández said. "When I was ready to quit it was probably selection number six. I was married by that time and my wife gave me a pep talk I'll never forget. She said that she believed in me. Her parting words were 'I don't know what they have that you don't have.'"

By that point, Hernandez said that he had already been through graduate school and did everything required by NASA. So, when his wife made that comment he started looking for the answer to why others were getting selected but he wasn't.

"I took a deep dive into everybody's curriculum – the folks who got selected (when) I didn't," Hernández said. "I compared them and yes they were a similar age as me, with similar education backgrounds, and similar work experience- but they were all pilots and I wasn't. So I thought maybe I should invest in myself and become a private pilot."

And that's exactly what Hernández said he did- he became a pilot. Next, he saw that the people selected by NASA were scuba dive-rated. He also learned that an international space station was in the process of being built in partnership with Russia. So Hernández upped the ante again by getting master-rated in scuba diving and becoming fluent in the Russian language.

After Hernández's 12th application with NASA, he said he was finally accepted, joining the program's 19th class of Astronauts in 2004. Four years later, his dream came true when he blasted off via rocket as a flight engineer and headed to outer space.

Hernández was a mission specialist on Space Shuttle Discovery's Mission STS-128 in August and September of 2009.

"It was a surreal experience. You can train as much as you want on Earth, but the real experience isn't real until it's real," Hernández said. "You never get tired of floating in space. It was just a great experience. Words cannot do it justice."

NASA's 19th class of Astronauts featuring Jose Hernández/ Courtesy of NASA

After Hernández left NASA, he wrote multiple books which prompted filmmakers to reach out with inquiries about turning his story into a movie. Multiple offers and negotiations later, Hernández said he decided to help create "A Million Miles Away" for Amazon Prime.

The movie premiered in late August in Stockton, the city that Hernández still calls home.

Hernández said that he hopes that after people watch "A Million Miles Away," they'll be encouraged to follow their dreams and know that they can do anything they put their minds to.

"It's a story of hard work, of education being the great equalizer, of the concept of the American Dream is alive and well if you're willing to work hard, persevere, and prepare yourself according to the challenge you select," said Hernandez at the premiere.

Tales of my immigrant Swedish grandmother

Attached is a copy of the little booklet prepared for the *"Celebration of life for Grandma Hedin."* My aunt Mill organized it.

Memories of our parents
Sarah Amanda and Olaf Mikael Hedin

I don't know the years our parents initially came to the United States, but we have copies of a post card received by our father in New Jersey in the year 1906 from a buddy, also living in the United Stated.

Although our parents were raised in the same village in Sweden, I don't believe they came to this country together. They were married in New York City in 1910 and settled in Seattle where our father (Papa) worked in the woods. I believe his last employment in the Pacific Northwest was with Weyhauser, his pay amounted to $2.00 per day and the "Company Store" recouped much of that.

Since I was born in Seattle in 1914, and Glady and Greta (twins) were born in Butte in 1916, our parents must have moved to Butte in the spring or summer of 1916.

Except for the deep affection he (Papa) had for his children, Papa's life seemed to be hell on earth in the last years of his life. He coughed continuously, since he had the "con", which was an abbreviated term for "consumption", currently known as silicosis. I believe his death certificate shows he died of pneumonia, bet he died of the "con".

I gave Papa his haircuts and he paid me a modest fee of what change he had in his pocket. His hair had turned green during those years. I recall Papa walking out to the ambulance for what turned out to be his last ride in an automobile. After the ambulance left, our mother told us that when Papa got well, we would be moving back to Sweden.

Papa's last employment was at the Elm Orlu mine, then owned by W.A. Clark. He died at age 47 in the year 1927. I was the oldest child at age 12, the youngest of six children was less than 11 months old.

Such a family situation was not at all atypical in those years.

Elmer Hedin

The following are some outstanding or humorous incidents from those who remember her, our Mom.

From Evert Hollbrink, in Sweden

Amanda took part in a horse race on the great Lake Starsjon on March 18th 1906. In that time in was an unusual event to find a woman handle a horse race. She was for certain a young, beautiful girl of character.

From Great Grand Son, Gary McHenry;

Being of a young age when Great Gramma Hedin left this world for a better place, this story comes from the generation who knew and loved her outlandish personality.

When I was about the age of five, my mother left me with Gramma for the day while she went shopping, as all young kids did, I had a habit of repeating things I heard, as we all know, Great Gramma had a language that sailors eventually developed and still use today. During my last visit, I repeated a word that apparently one not to be repeated by a 5 year old, for she washed by mouth out with soap. After I stopped crying and settled down some, I decided, if I couldn't use those words, then neither could she. If memory serves me correctly, it did not take long for her to start swearing at her knitting. I got the bar of soap out and washed her mouth out. This did not set well with her and I may not of sat too well either, for a few hours. I actually don't remember Great Gramma Hedin, not in a sad way, but in a way that I'm sure she would of wanted. This is a great way to pass on memories to future generations. I know I will tell my children about this wonderful person.

       Dedicated in loving memory of Amanda Hedin.

From Gulie Persson in Sweden:

Many of us still remember Amanda and all the good laughs we had, as she was a great character.

Our Mom was born October 25, 1887. Her name was Sarah Amanda Johnson. She came to New York in 1906 with a lady who later became her sister-in-law. She worked for awhile before going back to Sweden. After coming back and marrying our pa and settling in Seattle, she worked in a hospital before and after Elmer was born. She often told me of helping to keep a new born baby alive by breast feeding it.

When they first arrived in Butte, they moved into a house in the "Cabbage Patch" which wasn't too far from the red light district. One night some guy tried to climb through the window. Pa chased him down the street in his underwear and bare feet. He suddenly realized he wasn't dressed and gave up the chase. When Mom was alone, she was so frightened she pushed the furniture against the door.

Then they moved to a duplex just above Front Street where the twins Glady's and Greta were born. They lived there until Pa built a two story house on the flats where Doris, Ellen and myself were born.

After Pa's death, Mom went to work at Hanssen Packing Plant. She would take Doris and Ellen, to the neighbors to baby sit them while she was at work. Many times she hiked through the cold and deep snow to get there. Other times, one of the older children would take her in the horse and buggy. She finally got a car, a Model T, I think. It was nice, but she still had problems. The radiator would freeze up and she would cover it up with blankets and run it till it thawed out.

Mom always had a cow, a horse, and dogs. She also had pigs in later years. She would plant a garden every spring and when she couldn't plow the garden spot herself, she would hire Mac Namara, who I'm sure some of you remember.

Mom made several trips to Sweden. Two of her trips were very traumatic. She and our sister Gladys spent some time in Sweden, and returned on the last ship across when the Korean [world] War started. The ship was blacked out all the way across and took a round about way in fear of hitting mines in the ocean. They arrived in Butte on Christmas Eve.

In 1956, Mom and my daughter Millie were on the Swedish ship, the Andrea Doria, on June 23. They came back to Butte, then left again and stayed for eight years in Sweden.

We lost Gladys at age 53 on December 5, 1969 and Mom spent the rest of her life in the house that Pa build. We lost her October 2, 1974.

Mildred Hedin Ignatowiz

This incident must happened in the summer of 1923 or 1924. We kids were dutifully seated in our 1922 Model T Ford touring car which was parked outside of the Quinn's place. Our mother was inside swapping naughty stories with Mrs. Quinn and her oldest daughter, Frances. We kids were not allowed to listen to those stories.

One of the women looking out the kitchen window, spotted the black touring car which the Dry Squad used when it was conducting a raid. I don't recall weather the car was a Cadillac or a Pierce-Arrow.

The Dry Squad was responsible for the enforcement of the liquor that is, moonshine. Jerry Murphy and Ben Holter were two of the Dry Squad whom I recall. The name of the third escapes me.

The women correctly surmised that the Dry Squad was looking for our place. Frances and our mother ran through the field to our place, rolled the barrels of mash out to the yard and dumped the mash. The officers, of course, were expected to believe that the mash was for the pigs. The Dry Squad reached our place and the search was conducted for the still - how can one make moonshine without a still? I must now digress and point out that the outhouse was the first of the outbuilding to come into view as our place was approached. (I always felt it was more prominent than it should of been, regarding its end, I believe it was Ben Holter who headed for the outhouse. At this point Mrs. Quinn, who had been watching all of the proceedings from her front porch yelled out in her Irish brogue: "Jesus Christ, they're even looking in the shit-house.

Elmer Hedin

From Ruby Milligan Kinsfather:

When I was eight to ten years old, Amanda drove up to Silver St. She drove the old black horse and buggy and it was in the dead of winter. She tied the horse in the back and put six or eight caps on his ears and covered him with coats, then proceeded to party with Catherine and Jimmy Lane.

I also remember going up to your place many times for Ted, and he would find them drinking home brew and etc. Gramma Milligan would be so mad, she could have chewed nails. When she'd get him home, he would sneak off again to party and drink.

I also remember the time Amanda shut the oven door and built a fire in the range and roasted the kitten that was inside.

From Lucille Doyle Smigle:

Mandy and Uncle Jim were at the White Swan drinking a beer and dining on hard boiled eggs. Mandy's egg stuck in her throat and caused her to choke. In a voice you could hear she cried "get me the hell out of here and let me die in the country."

From Frances Doyle Mykanen:
The Midnight Ride of Mandy and Jim.

It was late at night the stars were out and so were Mandy and Uncle Jim. She stopped to pick up the evening paper. With her foot on the clutch, she reached out the door and, lo and behold, she fell out. The car took off with a jerk and she hollered to Uncle Jim, "Step on the brake, you !!!!!??. Instead, the gas pedal, he floored, and off through the field, like a big assed bird, he went. She chased him until the motor died of exhaustion right up against the Doyles bedroom. He was laughing so had he couldn't hear the cussing she gave him. All he could say was he saved the Doyles lives. Amen

From Joan Hennelly:

One thing I remember about Gramma Hedin was when John and I visited her Sweden.

The first time I met her she was a sleep on a bed by the window. She had been reading and the book slipped off her lap. She woke up and but it back across her stomach, but what was so funny were the cuss words she said in the process. I laughed so hard. She could swear and it never sounded bad. What a wonderful lady. We sure loved her.

Under the present circumstances, am sure I won't be able to attend that Special Hedin Reunion. However, am sure I'll hear the laughter and fun clear in Olympia.

The first time I met your Mom was in 1973 when Ev and I took Elmer up to the airport for the trip to Sweden. That's when I met all of you wonderful Hedins (by birth) and we waited most of the day before putting Amanda, Mikael and Elmer on the plane. From what Elmer told me, they offered double drinks for everyone - so she had a double Vodka and everyone enjoyed the trip. (Especially Amanda!)

From what I hear everyone on that flight raved about Mikael who was so devoted to his great grandmother.

When they left Skuko she smuggled some potato starts in her purse. From those seed potatoes she gave us some and the next summer we had a bumper crop of 'Swedish Potatoes." (Ev said they were blue?)

The next time we saw her was on my first trip to Butte. When we arrived she and Millie were making "Potato Sausage" Elmer's favorite. I was impressed with how she broke up the seasonings (large chunks) by pounding them and tasting the sausage until it satisfied her. She gave us some when we left and said she would send some occasionally via plane. (She died the next year.)

We did make a quick trip to see her when she was in the hospital - and she said, "How's Gary?" How she loved him.

I remember how each child of each generation was special to her and how she would sneak some money to each one.

How proud she was of each of the children whom she raised without welfare after your father passed away. You are all very talented, intelligent and so thoughtful and kind to everyone you meet. My friends and family are all impressed with your sense of humor, your ready laughter, and fun.

I don't know if anyone else has mentioned how clever your mother was. Some examples told to me were:

After Elmer became an Actuary she said, "Now you've got a bankers belly."

She also said, "I'd rather borrow from Elmer cause then I don't have to pay it back."

Have a good time at the reunion. I know you've put in a lot of hours planning such a big undertaking.

I would have had a Champagne lunch to kick off - so drink one for me.

You have been my family for almost 19 years and often you, my sister, were closer than my own. However, this is not written in sadness, but gladness for all the years we shared.

Mema

This is an open invitation to each of you to come visit me anytime. Like Ev always says, "Mern invited me to diner and I stayed 12 years."

From Mildred

Mom used to have a route she took each day to get food for the pigs. One place was Eddy's bakery, to get the left over bread dough and day old rolls, bread and etc. After getting the bag's of dough, one very warm day, she decided to stop at the White Swan to have her beer. After being there awhile, a friend came in and said, "Geez, Mandy, it's sure snowing out." She answered, "You're crazy." He said, "Go look at your truck," and when she did the dough had risen and hung almost down to the ground on both sides.

Another summer day, she brought some raisin bread dough home and fed it to the pigs. The raisins fermented and they got drunk and passed out. Ugh! I wonder if they had hang-overs.

One night after dark she took a wide turn off of Harrison Ave. and went half way into the basement where the Bungalow used to be. She got out and walked home. When she saw the car the next day, it was teetering. How lucky she was. That was close.

One evening after work she stopped at Doyles. It was dark when she left and she didn't know they had plowed the road and left a big trench. She hit that and ended up with two black eyes.

Greta Johnson

    We used to go with Mom to get gas and groceries. She got her gas from a good friend, on Harrison Ave., the Petersons. Mrs. Peterson was a very good cook - always made cakes, cookies, etc. she'd offer something to us kids. Of course we were bashful as kids so bashful we couldn't even say yes or no to the cake or whatever. Mom would answer for us it was always, "No they don't want any." We, as kids were so bashful - what ever happened to us? - we were so shy. I'm still the most timid of them all- (oink, oink)

    Ramona and I went shopping with Mom -Christmas time . We came upon this table of wigs on display there Mom looks them over and said I think I'll buy one and put it (beep or tween) my legs. I went one way and Mona went another. I said to her she's your mother not mine. All in all, she was a great mother.

    I remember Dad (Papa) we called him. One time to get groceries. He make us promise to stay home while they were gone. When they got back, we were gone. So he chased us in the house and we ran upstairs and he let us have it. He wanted us to be honest. What happened to us? since then.

From Doris

She and Wayne took Mom to Hamilton to the Doctor. When she had to fill out the usual papers. When she came to the part that said she wouldn't hold them responsible if she became sterile, she told the nurse, she wasn't going to sign it. The nurse asked her why and she said "Cause I don't want to become sterile." She was only 74.

When we were small, Mom used to get up in the morning and make dresses to go to school in. When we lost her and were going through her things, we found a slip that had safety pins all around the bottom to hold the hem up.

If she has a run or a hole in her black stockings, which she wore most of the time, she would put stove polish on her leg.

When Mom went somewhere special she put flour on her face. She then put on her hat and said, "Gosh, I look like a cat without ears."

One cold night she drained the radiator and the next morning she found a duck with his feet frozen in the ice.

Mom always had a problem with her animals - her goat chewed the top off of her car, and she had geese that chased cars and people.

She said to one of her kids "Get that book out of the car." When asked what the name of the book was she said, "Threes Crows in Boston," The name was really, "A Tree Grows in Brooklyn."

and Gramma told us jokes one right after another never telling the same on twice. (Wish I could just remember on of them) After a fashion we realized Gramma was not only entertaining us, but also our neighbors. They were out on their deck and enjoying all they heard. None of the jokes she told ever sounded dirty. We enjoyed her so and Alan couldn't believe this cute old lady was so full of fun, bull, pee and vinegar.

    The next visit was when I moved to Butte with 3 children and another in the oven. I was helping Millie do laundry as she had a broken arm, while helping her, I got my own done. Being sensitive, something that was said to one of my children upset me so that I was packing my stuff in the car to leave. Gramma said to Millie, "What the hells the matter with her." Millie didn't know as I probably didn't either. So Gramma said to me. "If you'd have a beer every day you wouldn't lose your mind." This was said with concern on her part. Ha Ha. The she asked if I'd give her a ride home. With in 5 blocks to pick up my tire that I'd gotten fixed, I had bad labor pains. Rather than tell Gramma I started back to Millies. She said, "Jesus Christ. Now I know you lost your mind you just left there." At that time I had to tell her. I was having pains. She said, "Oh, shit, you best pull over, I know you're a good driver but you better stop." I assured her I was fine. I pulled up at Millies and my crippled Gramma jumped out, left her cane in the car and was in the house before I could shut the car off telling everyone the baby was coming. My cousin Earl McLean came out telling me he'd take me to the hospital. I told him I had to talk to the kids before going as I never left them. So I went in Millies, sat down to tell my children I'd be gone away to bring back a brother or sister. Chris was saying, "No Mamma not today. Do it tomorrow." At this point Gramma said. "I'll be go to hell Earl. Go get us something to drink." What a gal. She'd never remember how many she'd had.

    I'm sure we all remember so much, but to put it on paper is hard. All I know is she put a lot of love, laughter and humor in our lives. I thank God each day for her and the family we have.

Darlene Butler
    My memories of my Grandmother Amanda Hedin

    My first memory of Gramma was when she came back from Sweden. I didn't recall ever seeing her before and I was so bashful and maybe even afraid of her. I'd look around the door jam and thought "Who is this woman." and what is she doing here. At this time she brought me (along with other grandchildren) a gold locket. It was so beautiful and I felt so special.

    My memories of Gramma were many. One thought I have is how she loved her grandchildren, and tolerated us so well. Her home was ours and we could do as we pleased. We were allowed to walk on the piano keys and play the piano at great length with no real music but lots of noise. No one dared tell us to stop either. My aunt Glady's also had this tolerance and had adopted Gramma's ways that as long as we weren't hurting ourselves or others we could so most anything. So fortunately it was a wonderful place for us children to be. Thank God for that.

    Gramma also made sure we had a bag of bread from Eddy's Bakery. On occasion it had other goodies included. Was like Christmas when she'd arrive.

    One day I went with Gramma and she stopped at the D. & M. Bar. She told me to sit in the car and not to get out, so I did. I being a little girl felt like I'd been there forever. I fell asleep off and on and was frightened because of strangers (maybe even drunks). Finally I asked a man and wife if they knew my Gramma Hedin. They said yes and went and told her I wanted her. She had forgot I was there and bawled me out cause I didn't come in sooner. She then took me in the bar, I was seated in a booth and she along with friends kept buying me pop and candy. With each item they bought me, I'd wanted one for my brother and sister which ended up being a lot.

    Another memory was when I lived in Grants Pass, Oregon. I was very much in the family way with my son Chris. Mom and John had taken Gramma, my husband Allan and myself to dinner. We went to a nice restaurant and waitress brought the food and said, "How was everything." We replied fine except for Gramma, she replied, "The noodles were good but ya need a magnifying glass to find the God damn turkey."

    We laughed but she didn't crack a smile.

    This same visit I lived in a duplex on the Rogue River. My neighbors were very religious (very nice also). It was probably 100° out and Gram, Mom and John were miserable. We sat on the deck all day

From Ellen Hardle

Hellen and Bill came out to the house and Mom was sitting next to Jack Collins talking to him and she turns to them and said, "The son of a BITCH can't hear a word I'm saying."

Cliff mentioned the time she took us out to the Teddy Bear for a picnic and ran into the ditch.

Mom would send us out when she saw someone coming, an insurance man or someone she didn't want to see to say she wasn't home. Then she would come out after we would tell them she wasn't home. Quite embarrassing huh!

I didn't attend Gramma's Celebration of Life; I don't recall knowing of it at the time.

But here are my thoughts about my gramma.

Amanda Hedin

Here I turn to my own personal heritage to find a hero.

This is my grandmother, a Swedish immigrant. She is one of my heroes because of who she was in the upbringing of my mother and aunts and an uncle during the Great depression.

I never knew my grandfather, he died of the Miners Conn, a lung disease common among hard rock miners. My mother was 12 years old and her and her twin sister Gladys took on the role of raising the younger sisters. Grandma did what so many women did in those days, and still do today – she did what she had to do to provide food, shelter, and clothing for her children. They lived in a small house and a few acres at the edge of town, and Grandma raised pigs, goats, chickens, geese – and of course kids. And she made moonshine during prohibition.

She drove her old cars around town gathering slop from restaurants and bakeries to feed the pigs. She swamped the bars around the off-shift miners. There was a custom in those days – if a bar customer dropped a coin on the floor, he was told "leave it for the swamper." Times were very tough in those days, but Gramma persevered. One of her old cars would only turn one direction, so she planned her route around Butte accordingly.

Mom's older brother Elmer used to visit in later years and sit at the kitchen table telling stories of those days. He was a good storyteller, and we were captivated by his tales. But he would always end by telling of how tough the times were back then. He often ended by telling us how the family did not know if or when the next meal might come or what it would be.

Yes, Grandma is a hero to me – as are so many that came through those times to become the Greatest Generation.

Immigration – yes, but with great care in culling out those who mean harm.

Ethnic Butte Montana

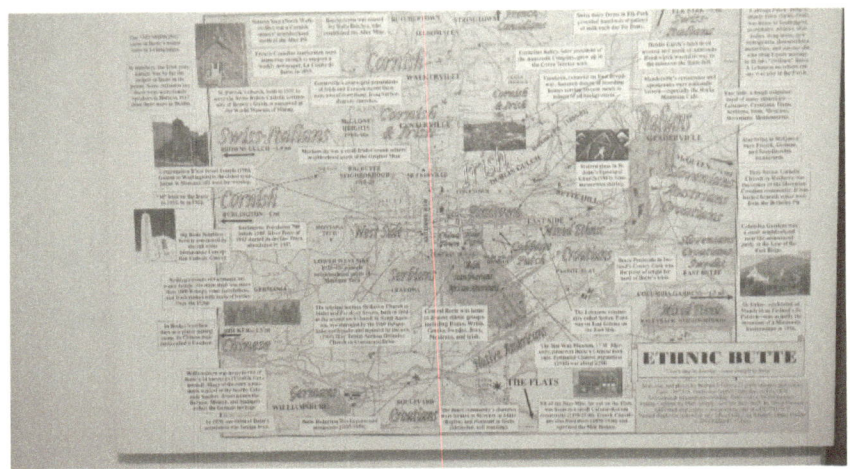

My hometown of Butte Montana is a microcosm of what immigration and assimilation has been in the history of America. The map above shows the various ethnic groupings on and surrounding the *"Richest Hill on Earth."* People came to Butte because that's where work was to be found. Some such as William A. Clark became very wealthy, but most fell into the working class and raised families on miners' wages and income from the various supporting stores and industries necessary for life in this mining city. My father worked for years at a meat packing plant, and later started his own business as a TV repairman.

Immigration and assimilation in places such as Butte is vividly illustrated by NO SMOKING signs posted in the mines – in 14 languages.

For the most part, the various ethnic groups assimilated well into the life blood of Butte. There were tensions and outbreaks of violence, but for the most part the violence was between the "Company" and the miners. Over time, the minors formed various unions as they sought economic advancement and protection against company abuse. Strikes were commonplace, and at times violence broke out. But I think you will be hard pressed to find the Serbs rising up against the Swedes, or the Irish invading the domains of the Italians. Such incursions did occur, but most often was found in marriages, such as a wedding of that Croat lady and an Irish lad – family cousins of this author.

What you will find in Butte is pride. The pride of the Serbs as manifested beautifully in the Serbian Orthodox Church on the East Side. The Pride of the Irish and Italian Catholic community as shown in the extensive Catholic school system and the many churches. The pride that each ethnic community has in its history and traditions.

And covering these many pockets of pride is the covering of a pride in Butte and its history, traditions, and cultures.

About the author

Don Johnson was raised in Butte, Montana and joined the Navy in 1964 at 20 years of age. Following his years of active duty, including a tour to the Vietnam war zone in 1966, he finished college with a degree in mathematics from San Diego State University and entered the field of software development.

Don's connection with the Navy did not end at the completion of his enlistment. For many years after his destroyer assignments, he was a software developer at Cubic Defense Systems, slinging code for the US Navy & Air Force Tactical Aircrew Combat Training System (TACTS/ACMI), the premier online training system for US and allied combat aircrews.

Don has a lifelong interest in history, politics and current events which is reflected in his writings. In recent years, Don has experienced a rekindling of interest in his Navy service and has reconnected with shipmates from his old ship by joining the USS Balch/Porterfield Reunion Association.

Don's books can be found at
https://www.amazon.com/author/donjohnsonbooks

And his thoughts on a variety of topics can be found at his blog:

https://ayearningforpublius.wordpress.com/

www.ingramcontent.com/pod-product-compliance
Lightning Source LLC
Chambersburg PA
CBHW021409210526
45463CB00001B/289